DICTIONARY
OF
MYTHOLOGY

DICTIONARY
OF
MYTHOLOGY

BY

P. G. Woodcock

PHILOSOPHICAL LIBRARY

New York

Copyright 1953 by Philosophical Library, Inc.,
200 West 57th Street, New York, N. Y. 10019
Reprinted 1981
All rights reserved
ISBN 8022-1927-6
Manufactured in the United States of America

DICTIONARY
OF
MYTHOLOGY

A

Abas, son of Meganira, who was turned into a water-lizard, for disparaging the ceremonial of the Sacrifice.

Absyrtus, brother of Medea.

Abydos, city of Asia famous for the loves of Hero and Leander, and for the bridge of boats built by Xerxes across the Hellespont. Leander constantly swam across the Hellespont to see Hero until, on a stormy night, he was drowned. See "The Bride of Abydos," Byron.

Abydos, a town in Egypt famous for the temple of Osiris.

Academia, place near Athens surrounded with trees, belonging to Academus, from whom the name was derived. Plato opened his school of philosophy here, thus giving the name of Academia to places of sacred learning.

Achates, friend of Aeneas, whose faithfulness was such that FIDUS ACHATES has become a proverb.

Achelous, son of Oceanus and Terra, or Tethys, god of the river of the same name in Epirus. He was one of the many suitors of Dejanira, entering the lists against Hercules, and finding himself inferior changed his body into a serpent, and later into an ox. Hercules broke off one of his horns and defeated him, after which it has been said, he was changed into a river.

Achilles, son of Peleus and Thetis, and the bravest Greek in the Trojan War. During infancy Thetis plunged him into the Styx, so making every part of his body invulnerable except the heel by which she held him. To prevent his going to the Trojan War, Thetis sent him to the court of Lycomedes, where he was disguised as a woman. As Troy could not be taken without his aid,

3

Ulysses went to the court in the dress of a merchant, and offered jewels and arms for sale. Achilles chose the arms, thus revealing his sex, and went to the war. Vulcan made him a strong suit of armour, proof against all weapons. Agamemnon deprived him of his favourite Briseis, and for this affront he would not appear on the field until the death of Patroclus impelled him to vengeance. He slew Hector, who had killed Patroclus, and tied his corpse to his war-car, dragging it three times round Troy. He is said to have been killed by Paris, who inflicted a mortal wound in his vulnerable heel with an arrow.

Acis, a Sicilian shepherd, son of Faunus and the nymph Simaethis. He was passionately loved by Galatea but his rival, Polyphemus, crushed him to death with a piece of rock. The gods changed Acis into a stream, which rises from Mt. Aetna.

Actaeon, famous huntsman, son of Aristaeus and Autonoe, daughter of Cadmus. He saw Diana and her attendants bathing, for which he was changed into a stag and eaten by his own dogs.

Actium, town and promontory of Epirus, famous for the naval victory of Augustus over Antony and Cleopatra, B.C. 31.

Ades or Hades, the god of Hell amongst the Greeks equalling the Pluto of the Latins. The word is often used for Hell itself by ancient poets.

Adherbal, son of Micipsa, and grandson of Masinissa. He was besieged at Cirta, and put to death by Jugurtha, after imploring the aid of Rome in vain (B.C. 112).

Admetus, son of Pheres and Clymene, king of Pherae in Thessaly. Apollo is said to have tended his flocks for nine years after being banished from heaven.

Adonis, son of Cinyras and Myrrha, he was the favourite of Venus. Being fond of hunting, he slighted the advice not to hunt wild beasts and was mortally wounded by a wild boar. Venus changed him into an anemone. Proserpine restored him to life on condition that he spend six months in the year with her and the rest with Venus. See Shakespeare's poem "Venus and Adonis."

Adrastaea, another name for Nemesis, one of the goddesses of justice.

Adrastus, son of Talaus and Lysimache. He was king of Argos. Polynices, being banished from Thebes by his brother Eteocles, fled to Argos, where he married Argia, daughter of Adrastus. The king assisted him with an army against Thebes. He was defeated and fled to Athens, where Theseus helped him and was victorious. Adrastus died from grief for the death of his son Aegialeus.

Adrianus, famous Emperor of Rome, who was a learned, warlike and austere general. He came to Britain and built a wall between what are now known as Carlisle and Newcastle-on-Tyne, to protect the Britons from the raids of the Caledonians.

Adscripticii Dii, gods of the second grade.

Aeacus, one of the judges of hell, with Minos and Rhadamanthus.

Aecastor, an oath used only by women, referring to the Temple of Castor.

Aedepol, an oath used by both men and women, referring to the Temple of Pollux.

Aediles, Roman magistrates, who had charge of all buildings, baths, and aqueducts, and weights and measures. They held an honourable office leading to a more distinguished position in the State.

Aegeon, giant with fifty heads and a hundred hands, who was imprisoned by Jupiter beneath Mt. Aetna.

Aegeus, King of Athens, son of Pandion. Desiring children, he went to consult an oracle and returning stopped at the court of Pittheus, king of Troezene, who gave him his daughter Aethra in marriage. He directed her, if she had a son, to send him to Athens as soon as he could lift a stone under which he had concealed his sword. Aethra became mother of Theseus, whom she sent to Athens with his father's sword, Aegeus being at that time living with Medea, the divorced wife of Jason. When Theseus arrived at Athens, Medea attempted to poison him but he escaped. He showed Aegeus the sword thus discovering himself to be his son. When Theseus returned from Crete, after the death of the Minotaur, he omitted to hoist white sails, as a signal of success, and at sight of black sails, Aegeus, concluding that his son was dead, threw himself into the sea, which has since been called the Aegean Sea. Aegeus died B.C. 1235.

Aegis, the shield of Jupiter, so called because it was made of goat skin. He gave it to Pallas, who placed Medusa's head on it, which turned into stone all who gazed at it.

Aegle, the fairest of the Naiads.

Aegyptus, son of Belus, and brother of Danaus. He gave his fifty sons in marriage to the fifty daughters of his brother. Danaus, who had established himself at Argos and was jealous of his brother, obliged all his daughters to murder their husbands on the first night of their nuptials, but Hypermnestra spared her husband Lynceus. Aegyptus was killed by Polyxena, his niece.

Aelianus Claudius, Roman sophist of Praeneste in the reign of Adrian who taught rhetoric at Rome. He wrote seventeen books relating to animals and fourteen on various subjects. He died A.D. 140 at the age of sixty.

Aello, one of the Harpies.

Aeneas, Trojan prince, son of Anchises and Venus. He married Creusa, daughter of Priam, and they had a son named Ascanius. During the Trojan war, Aeneas showed the greatest courage in defence of Troy. When the city was in flames, he carried his father on his shoulders and led his son Ascanius by the hand, while his wife followed. Later he built twenty ships with which he sailed in quest of a settlement. The wind drove him to the coast of Africa where he was kindly received by Dido, Queen of Carthage, who fell in love with him; but he left Carthage by order of the gods. The term "Pius" is often appended to his name on account of his submission to the gods.

Aeneis, the Aeneid, a poem by Virgil of well-known merit. The author imitated the style of Homer, whom some thought he equalled.

Aeolus, god of the winds. Jupiter was his supposed father, and his mother was said to be a daughter of Hippotus. Aeolus is reputed to have had the power to hold the winds confined in a cavern, occasionally giving them liberty to blow over the world. When Ulysses visited him on his return from Troy he gave him, tied in a bag, all the winds that could prevent his voyage being prosperous. The companions of Ulysses, surmising that the bag contained treasure, cut it open within sight of Ithaca, the port for which they were making; the contrary winds rushed out and drove back the ship for many leagues. Aeolus lived at Strongyle, now named Strombolo.

Aeschines, Athenian orator living about 342 B.C. He was distinguished for his rivalship with Demosthenes.

Aeschylus, soldier poet of Athens, son of Euphorion. He fought at Marathon, Salamis, and Plataea, but he was most famous for his writings. He wrote ninety tragedies, for forty of which he received a public prize. He was killed by a tortoise falling from the beak of an eagle and striking his head, in B.C. 456.

Aesculapius, the god of physic, was son of Apollo and Coronis, or some suppose Larissa, daughter of Phlegias. He was physician to the Argonauts in their expedition to Colchis. He became so famous that Pluto became jealous and asked Jupiter to kill him with a thunder-bolt. To revenge his death Apollo slew the Cyclops who had forged the missile. By a marriage with Epione he had two sons, Machaon and Podalirus, both famous physicians, and four daughters, of whom Hygeia, goddess of health, is most renowned. Many temples were erected in honour of Aesculapius, in which votive tablets were hung by people who had recovered from sickness. His most famous shrine was at Epidaurus, where, every five years, games took place in his honour. He is variously represented, but his most famous statue shows him seated on a throne of gold and ivory, his head crowned with rays and wearing a long beard. A knotty stick is in one hand, and a staff entwined with a serpent in the other, while a dog lies at his feet.

Aeson, son of Cretheus and twin of Pelias. He succeeded his father as king of Iolchos, but was soon exiled by his brother. He married Alcimeda, who bore him Jason, whose education he entrusted to Chiron. When Jason grew up he demanded his father's kingdom from his uncle, who gave him evasive answers and persuaded him to go in quest of the Golden Fleece. On his return Jason found his father very infirm, and at his request Medea drew the blood from Aeson's veins and refilled them with the juice of certain herbs which restored him to the vigour of youth.

Aesopus, Phrygian philosopher, was originally a slave. He procured his liberty by his genius and dedicated his fables to his patron Croesus. The book known as Aesop's fables today is a collection of fables and apologues of wits before and after the age of Aesopus.

Aeta, king of Colchis, and father of Medea.

Agamemnon, king of Mycene and Argos, was brother to Menelaus, and son of Plisthenes, the son of Atreus. He married Clytemnestra, and Menelaus Helen, both daughters of Tyndarus, king of Sparta. When Helen eloped with Paris, Agamemnon was elected commander-in-chief of the Grecian forces invading Troy.

Aganippides, a name of the Muses, derived from the fountain of Aganippe.

Agesilaus, of the family of Proclidae, son of Archidamus, king of Sparta, whom he succeeded. He made war against Artaxerxes, king of Persia. He was successful but in the midst of his conquests he was recalled to oppose the Athenians and Boeotians. It took him thirty days to pass the tract of country which had taken a whole year of Xerxes' expedition. He defeated his enemies at Coronea, but sickness interfered with his conquests, and the Spartans were beaten in all battles until he again appeared at their head. He died 362 B.C.

Agineus, see Apollo.

Aglaia, one of the Three Graces.

Agni, Hindoo god of lightning.

Agrippa, M. Vipsanius, celebrated Roman who obtained victory over S. Pompey, and espoused the cause of Augustus at the battles of Actium and Philippi, where he fought with great bravery. In his expeditions in Gaul and Germany he obtained several victories, but refused the honour of a triumph, and turned his attention to the beautifying of Rome; he built the Pantheon. Augustus gave him his daughter Julia in marriage. He died B.C. 12 aged 51.

Agrippa, son of Aristobulus, grandson of Herod the Great. The

Jews flattered him with the appellation of god and it is said that while they were so doing he was struck dead, A.D. 43. His son of the same name was with Titus at the siege of Jerusalem and died A.D. 94. It was before him that St. Paul pleaded. There were others less well known of the same name.

Ajax, one of the bravest of the Greek warriors in the Trojan war. He was son of Telamon and Eriboea. Some attribute his death to Ulysses, others say he was killed by Paris. Yet others assert that he went mad after being defeated by Ulysses, and committed suicide. Another Ajax was son of Oileus; he also took a prominent part in the Trojan war.

Alaricus, famous king of the Goths who plundered Rome in the reign of Honorius. He was renowned for valour, and during his reign he kept the Roman Empire in continual alarm. He died when he had reigned for twelve years in A.D. 410. He was buried in the bed of a river which had been turned from its course for that purpose, in order that it might be said that no one should tread on the earth where he rested.

Albion, son of Neptune and Amphitrite, came to Britain where he established a kingdom, and introduced astrology, and the art of building ships. Great Britain is sometimes called "Albion" after him.

Alcaeus, lyric poet of Mitylene in Lesbos about 600 years before the Christian era. He fled from battle and the armour he left in the field was hung in the temple of Minerva as a monument of his disgrace. He was enamoured of Sappho. Only a few fragments of his works remain.

Alceste, or Alcestis, daughter of Pelias, married Admetus. With her sisters she put her father to death that Medea might restore him to youth and vigour. This she had promised but refused later, on which the sisters fled to Admetus, who married Alceste.

Alcibiades, Athenian general, famous for his enterprise, genius, and natural foibles. He was a disciple of Socrates whose lessons and example had a steadying influence on his vicious propensities. In the Peloponnesian war he encouraged the Athenians to undertake an expedition against Syracuse. He died B.C. 404 aged 46.

Alcides, one of the names of Hercules.

Alcmena, daughter of Electrion, king of Argos. Her father promised her and his crown to Amphitryon if he would revenge the death of his sons who had been killed by the Teleboans. In the absence of Amphitryon, Jupiter assumed his form and visited Alcmena, who, believing the god to be her lover, received him with joy. Amphitryon on his return learned from the prophet Tiresias the deception that had been practised. After the death of Amphitryon, Alcmena married Rhadamanthus. Hercules was the son of Jupiter and Alcmena.

Alcyone, or Halcyone, daughter of Aeolus, married Ceyx, who was drowned as he was going to consult the oracle. The gods told Alcyone in a dream of her husband's fate; when she found his body washed ashore she threw herself into the sea, and she and her husband were changed into birds.

Alecto, one of the Furies, depicted with her head covered with serpents, and breathing pestilence, war, and vengeance.

Alectryon, servant of Mars, who changed him into a cock because he did not warn his master of the rising of the sun.

Alexander, surnamed the Great, son of Philip and Olympias. He was born B.C. 355, on the night on which the famous temple of Diana at Ephesus was burnt. This was prognostic, according to the magicians, of his future greatness and his taming of Bucephalus, a horse which none of the king's attendants could manage. Philip said, with tears in his eyes, that his son must seek another kingdom, as Macedonia would not be large enough for him. He built a town, which he called Alexandria, on the Nile. His conquests extended to India, where he fought with Porus, a powerful king of that country, and after he had invaded Syria, he returned to Babylon laden with spoils. His entry into this city was predicted by the magicians as proving fatal to him. He died in Babylon in his thirty-second year, after a reign of twelve years and eight months of continuous success, in B.C. 323. There were a number of others of the same name but less well known.

Alfadur, the Supreme Being, father of all, in Scandinavian mythology.

Alma Mammosa, a name of Ceres.

Alpheus, a river god. See Arethusa.

Altar, structure on which a sacrifice was offered. The earliest altars were just heaps of earth or turf or unhewn stone; as the mode of sacrificing became more ceremonious more elaborate altars were erected. Some were of marble and brass, decorated with carvings and bas-reliefs, having corners modelled as the heads of animals. They varied in height from two to four feet, and some were built solid; others were made hollow to retain the blood of the victims. Some were provided with a kind of dish, into which incense was thrown to overpower the smell of burning fat. This was probably the origin of the custom of burning incense at the altar.

Althaea, daughter of Thestius and Eurythemis, married Oeneus, king of Calydon, by whom she had many children, amongst them Meleager. When he was born the Parcae put a log on the fire, saying, as long as it was preserved the life of the child would be prolonged. The mother took the wood from the flames and preserved it, but when Meleager killed his two uncles, Althaea, to revenge them, threw the log into the fire, and when it was burnt Meleager died. Althaea killed herself.

Amalthaea, the goat which nourished Jupiter.

Amaryllis, name of a country woman in Virgil's Eclogues. Some have thought that the poet referred to Rome under this fictitious name.

Amazones, or Amazonides, nation of famous women who lived near the river Thermodon in Cappadocia. All spent their lives in wars and manly pursuits. They founded an empire in Asia Minor on the shores of the Euxine.

Ambarvalia, festivals in honour of Ceres, instituted by Roman husbandmen to purge their fields. At the spring festival the head of each family led an animal, usually a pig or ram, decked with oak boughs, round his fields, and offered milk and new wine. After harvest another festival was held at which Ceres was presented with the first fruits of the season. See Ceres.

Ambracia, city of Epirus, the home of King Pyrrhus. Augustus after the battle of Actium called it Nicopolis.

Ambrosia, Bacchanalian festivals.

Amica, a name of Venus.

Amphiaraus, son of Oicleus and Hypermnestra, was present at the chase of the Calydonian boar, and accompanied the Argonauts on their expedition. He was renowned for his knowledge of futurity.

Amphictyon, son of Deucalion and Pyrrha, reigned at Athens after Cranaus. Some say the deluge happened in his age.

Amphictyon, son of Helenus, who established the Council of the Amphictyons, composed of the wisest and most virtuous men of some of the cities of Greece.

Amphion, son of Jupiter and Antiope. He was skilled in music. It is said that at the sound of his lute, the stones arranged themselves so regularly as to form the walls of the city of Thebes.

Amphitrite, or Salatia, wife of Neptune and daughter of Oceanus and Terra. She was mother of Triton, a sea god.

Amphitryon, Theban prince, son of Alcaeus and Hipponome. His sister Anaxo married Electryon, king of Mycenae, whose sons were killed in battle by the Teleboans. Electryon gave his daughter Alcmena to Amphitryon for avenging the death of his sons.

Amycus, king of Babrycia, son of Neptune, killed by Pollux.

Anacharsis, Scythian philosopher 592 B.C., who, on account of his wisdom, temperance and knowledge, has been called one of the seven wise men. He was famous among the ancients for his writings, poems on war, and laws of the Scythians.

Anacreon, famous lyric poet of Teos, in Ionia. He was favoured by Hipparchus and Polycrates. Some of his odes are extant, and the elegance of his poetry has been admired in every age. He lived to be eighty-five and after a life of voluptuousness was choked with a grape pip. The odes have been translated into English by Moore, Cowley, and others.

Anadyomene, a famous painting of Venus by Apelles showing her rising from the sea.

Anaxagoras, Clazomenian philosopher, who disregarded wealth and honours to indulge his fondness for meditation and philosophy. He applied himself to astronomy, and obtained a knowledge of eclipses. He used to say he preferred a grain of wisdom to heaps of gold. He was accused of impiety and condemned to die, but he ridiculed the sentence, which he said had already been pronounced on him by nature. He died B.C. 428 at the age of seventy-two.

Anaxarete, a girl of Salamis, who so arrogantly rejected the addresses of Iphis, that he hanged himself at her door. She regarded this without emotion, and was changed into stone.

Ancaeus, son of Neptune, who left a cup of wine to hunt a boar which killed him, and the wine was left untasted. Thus the proverb, "There's many a slip 'twixt cup and lip."

Anchises, son of Capys and Themis, who was so beautiful that Venus came down from heaven on Mt. Ida to enjoy his company. Aeneas was the son of Anchises and Venus, and was entrusted to the care of Chiron the Centaur. When Troy was taken, Anchises had become so infirm that Aeneas had to carry him through the flames, thus saving his life.

Ancilia, the twelve sacred shields. The first Ancile was supposed to have fallen from heaven in answer to the prayer of Numa Pompilius. It was preserved with the greatest care, as it had been foretold that the fate of the Roman people would depend upon its safe keeping. Priests were appointed to take care of the Ancilia, and on the first of March each year the shields were carried in procession, and in the evening there was a feast called Coena Saliaris.

Andromache, daughter of Eetion, king of Thebes. She married Hector, son of Priam, and was mother of Astyanax. Her parting with Hector, who was going to battle, is described in the Iliad, and has been considered one of the most beautiful passages in that work.

Andromeda, daughter of Cepheus, king of Aethiopia. She was promised in marriage to Phineus. Neptune drowned the kingdom and sent a sea-monster to ravage the country, because Cassiope had boasted that she was more beautiful than Juno and the Nereides. The oracle of Jupiter Ammon was consulted, but nothing could stop the resentment of Neptune except the exposure of Andromeda to the sea-monster. She was therefore tied to a rock, but at the moment the monster was about to devour her, Perseus, returning from the conquest of the Gorgons, saw her, and was captivated with her beauty. He changed the monster into a rock by showing Medusa's head, and released Andromeda and married her.

Anemone, Venus changed Adonis into this flower.

Angeronia, or Volupia, was the goddess having power to dispel anguish of mind.

Anna Perenna, one of the rural divinities.

Antaeus, a giant vanquished by Hercules. Each time Hercules threw him the giant gained new strength from touching the earth, so Hercules lifted him from the ground and squeezed him to death.

Anteros, one of the two Cupids, sons of Venus.

Anthropophagi, a people of Scythia who fed on human flesh.

Anticlea, the mother of Ulysses.

Antigone, daughter of Oedipus, king of Thebes. She buried her brother Polynices by night against the order of Creon. He ordered her to be burned alive, but she killed herself on hearing the sentence. The death of Antigone is the subject of one of the finest tragedies of Sophocles.

Antigonus, one of Alexander's generals, who, after the division of the provinces after the king's death, received Pamphylia, Lycia, and Phrygia. His power became such that Ptolemy, Seleucus, Cassander, and Lysimachus combined to destroy him. He gained many victories over them but was at last killed B.C. 301 at the age of eighty. There were others of the same name but less well known.

Antinous, a youth of Bithynia of whom the emperor Adrian was so extremely fond that he erected a temple to him at his death, and wished it to be believed that he had been changed into a constellation.

Antiochus, surnamed Soter, son of Seleucus and king of Syria.

He made an alliance with Ptolemy Philadelphus, king of Egypt. He married his stepmother Stratonice. He was succeeded by his son Antiochus the Second, who put an end to the war which had begun with Ptolemy, and married his daughter Berenice, but being already married to Laodice, she, in revenge, poisoned him. Antiochus the third of that name, surnamed the Great, was king of Syria, and reigned thirty-six years. He was defeated by Ptolemy at Raphia. He conquered the greater part of Greece, and Hannibal incited him to enter on a campaign against Rome. He was killed B.C. 187. Antiochus Epiphanes, the fourth of the name, was king of Syria after his brother Seleucus. He behaved with cruelty to the Jews. He reigned eleven years and died unmourned. Others of the same name are less well known.

Antiope, was wife of Lycus, king of Thebes. Jupiter, disguised as a satyr, led her away and corrupted her.

Antipater, son of Iolaus, was a soldier under King Philip who was made a general under Alexander the Great. When Alexander invaded Asia, he left Antipater supreme governor of Macedonia. He has been suspected of giving poison to Alexander to advance himself in power.

Antoninus, surnamed Pius, was adopted by the Emperor Adrian whom he succeeded. He was noted for all the virtues, making a perfect statesman, philosopher, and king. He treated his subjects with humanity, and listened patiently to every complaint brought to his notice. He died A.D. 160 aged seventy-five after reigning twenty-three years.

Antoninus, Julius, son of Antony by Fulvia. He was consul with Paulus Fabius Maximus. He was surnamed Africanus, and was put to death by order of Augustus. (Some writers state that he killed himself.)

Antoninus, Marcus, Mark Antony the triumvir distinguished for ambitious views. When Caesar was killed in the senate house, Antony delivered an oration, the eloquence of which is recorded in Shakespeare's "Julius Caesar." Antony married Fulvia, whom he repudiated to marry Octavia, sister of Augustus. He fought on the side of Augustus at the battle of Philippi, against the murderers of Caesar. Later he became enamoured with Cleopatra, Queen of Egypt, and repudiated Octavia to marry her. He was defeated at the battle of Actium, and stabbed himself. He died B.C. 30 aged 56.

Antoninus, M. Gnipho, poet of Gaul who taught rhetoric at Rome. Cicero frequented his school. Others of the same name were of less repute.

Anubis, or Hermanubis, a god half a dog, a dog half a man, called Barker by Virgil and others.

Aonides, a name of the Muses, from the country Aonia.

Apelles, celebrated painter of Cos or possibly Ephesus. He was son of Pithius and lived in the age of Alexander the Great, who forbade any but Apelles to paint his portrait. He was so absorbed in his profession that he allowed no day to pass without exercising his art: hence the proverb, "Nulla dies sine linea." His most famous picture was Venus Anadyomene which was not quite finished when he died. He painted a picture of a horse, delineating it so perfectly that a passing horse neighed, supposing it to be alive. He was ordered by Alexander to paint a portrait of Campaspe. Apelles became enamoured with her and married her. He only put his name to three of his pictures, a sleeping Venus, Venus Anadyomene, and an Alexander. The proverb, "Ne sutor ultra crepidam," has been used in reference to him.

Aphrodite, the Grecian name for Venus, from the Greek *aphros*, froth, because Venus is said to have been born from the froth of the ocean.

Apicius, famous gourmand in Rome. Three of this name were all remarkable for voracious appetites.

Apis, name given to Jupiter by the people of the Lower Nile.

Apis, ancient king of Peloponnesus, son of Phoroneus and Laodice. Some say Apollo was his father and that he was king of Argos, others called him king of Sicyon. Varro amongst others has supposed that Apis went to Egypt with a colony of Greeks, and that he civilised the inhabitants and polished their manners, for which they made him a god after his death, and paid divine honours to him under the name of Serapis.

Apis, the miraculous ox worshipped in Egypt.

Apollo, famous god, sometime king of Arcadia, and son of Jupiter and Latona. He was known by many names but principally as Sol (the sun); Cynthius, from Mt. Cynthus in the Isle of Delos, his native place; Delius, from his birthplace; Delphinius, from his occasionally assuming the form of a dolphin; Delphicus, from his connection with the temple at Delphi, where he uttered the famous oracles. Some writers record that this oracle became dumb when Jesus Christ was born. Other common names of Apollo were Didymaeus, Nomius, Paean, and Phoebus. The Greeks called him Agineus because he was guardian of streets, and he was called Pythius from having slain the serpent Python. Apollo is usually represented as a handsome young man without beard, crowned with laurel, a bow in one hand and a lyre in the other. His favourite residence was on Mt. Parnassus, where he presided over the Muses. He was the accredited father of several children, the two best known being Aesculapius and Phaeton.

Apotheosis, the consecration of a god.

Appianus, historian of Alexandria flourishing A.D. 123. His Universal History, in twenty-four books, was the history of all nations conquered by the Romans.

Appius Claudius, a decemvir who obtained power by force and oppression. He grossly insulted Virginia, whom her father killed to save her from the power of this tyrant.

Apple, see Atalanta.

Arachne, Lydian princess who challenged Minerva to a spinning contest, but Minerva struck her on the head with a spindle, and turned her into a spider.

Arcadia, district of Peloponnesus, which has been much praised by poets. It was famous for its mountains. The people were mostly shepherds, who lived on acorns. They were skillful warriors and musicians. Pan lived among them.

Arcas, son of Calisto. He was turned into a he-bear and later into the constellation Ursa Minor.

Archer, see Chiron.

Archilochus, poet of Paros, who wrote elegies, satires, odes and epigrams, flourishing B.C. 685.

Archimedes, famous geometrician of Syracuse who invented a machine of glass that represented the motion of the heavenly bodies. When Marcellus, the Roman consul, besieged Syracuse, Archimedes constructed machines which suddenly raised into the air the enemy ships which then fell back and sank. He also set fire to the ships with burning glasses. When the enemy were in possession of a town, a soldier, not knowing who he was, killed him, B.C. 212.

Areopagitae, judges who sat at the Areopagus.

Areopagus, hill at Athens where Mars was tried for murder before twelve of the gods.

Ares, same as Mars, the god of war.

Arethusa, nymph of Elis, daughter of Oceanus, and an attendant on Diana. As she returned from hunting she bathed in the Alpheus stream. The god of the river was enamoured of her, and pursued her over the mountains till she was tired out. She implored Diana to change her into a fountain, which the goddess did.

Argo, the famous ship which carried Jason and his companions to Colchis, when they went to recover the Golden Fleece.

Argonautae, the Argonauts were ancient heroes, led by Jason, who went in the Argo to Colchis to recover the Golden Fleece, about seventy-nine years before the capture of Troy.

Argus, son of Arestor, he is sometimes called Arestorides. He had a hundred eyes of which only two were asleep at a time. Juno set him to watch Io, whom Jupiter had changed into a heifer, but Mercury, by order of Jupiter, slew him, by lulling all his eyes to sleep with music of the lyre. Juno put the eyes of Argus in the tail of a peacock, a bird sacred to her.

Ariadne, daughter of Minos, second king of Crete, and Pasiphae, fell in love with Theseus, who was shut up in the labyrinth to be devoured by the Minotaur. She gave Theseus a thread by which he could find his way out from the windings of the labyrinth. He conquered the Minotaur and married Ariadne, but later forsook her. Some say she hanged herself, others that Bacchus fell in love with her, giving her a crown of seven stars, which were made a constellation.

Arion, famous lyric poet and musician of Methymna, in Lesbos. He was son of Cyclops. He went to Italy with Periander, tyrant of Corinth, where he became rich by his arts. Afterwards, wishing to visit his birthplace, he embarked, but the crew decided to kill him for his riches. Arion entreated them to listen to his music, and as soon as it was finished, plunged into the sea. A number of dolphins had been attracted by his music, one of them carrying him safely back to Taenarus, whence he went to the court of Periander, who ordered the crew to be crucified.

Aristaeus, son of Apollo and Cyrene. He married Autonoe, daughter of Cadmus, Actaeon being their son. He was famous for his fondness for hunting; he also taught mankind the use of honey, and how to extract oil from olives. After his death he was worshipped as a demigod, presiding over trees.

Aristarchus, celebrated grammarian of Samos, disciple of Aristophanes. He lived most of his life at Alexandria. He wrote eight hundred commentaries on different authors. He died B.C. 157 aged seventy-two.

Aristides, celebrated Athenian, son of Lysimachus, in the days of Themistocles, whose temperance and virtue earned for him the name of the "Just." He was rival to Themistocles, by whose influence he was banished for ten years. He fought at Salamis and was appointed chief commander with Pausanias against Mardonius, whom they defeated at Platae.

Aristippus, the Elder, philosopher of Cyrene, disciple of Socrates, and founder of the Cyrenaic sect.

Aristogiton and Harmodius, two famous friends at Athens, who jointly delivered their country from the tyranny of Pisistratidae, B.C. 570.

Aristophanes, comic poet of Athens, son of Philip of Rhodes. He wrote fifty-four comedies, eleven of which we still have. He decried the vices of his times with a masterly pen. He flourished B.C. 434.

Aristoteles, famous philosopher, born at Stagira, son of Nicomachus. He went to Athens to hear Plato's lectures, soon signallising himself by his genius. Plato referred to him as the philosopher of truth, while Cicero complimented him for his eloquence and extensive knowledge. He died B.C. 322, aged sixty-three. As he lay dying he is reported to have said, "Causa causarum miserere mei"; this sentence has since become famous but some attribute it to Cicero. The term Stagirite has been applied to Aristoteles from the name of his native town.

Armata, one of the names of Venus, given to her by Spartan women.

Artaxerxes, the first successor to the throne of Persia after Xerxes. He fought against the Bactrians, and reconquered Egypt which had revolted. He was renowned for equity and moderation.

Artaxerxes, the Second, king of Persia, surnamed Mnemon. His brother Cyrus endeavoured to usurp him, marching against him at the head of 100,000 barbarians and 13,000 Greeks. Artaxerxes opposed him with a large army at Cunaxa, where Cyrus was killed and his men routed.

Artemis, Greek name of Diana. Her festivals, called Artemesia, were celebrated in Greece, particularly at Delphi.

Aruspices, sacrificial priests.

Ascalaphus, was changed into an owl, the forerunner of misfortune, by Ceres, because he told Pluto that Proserpina had eaten in the infernal regions, and thus prevented her return to earth.

Ascanius, son of Aeneas and Creusa, was rescued from the flames of Troy by his father, whom he accompanied in his voyage to Italy. He was later known as Iulus.

Ascolia, Bacchanalian feasts, from a Greek word meaning a leather bottle. The bottles were used to jump on at the games.

Asopus, son of Jupiter, killed by one of his father's thunderbolts.

Aspasia, daughter of Hermotimus and Phocea, renowned for her charm. She was priestess of the sun, and became mistress to Cyrus.

Assabinus, Ethiopian name of Jupiter.

Asses' ears, see Midas.

Astarte, powerful divinity of Syria, the same as the Venus of the Greeks. She had a famous temple at Hierapolis in Syria, which was attended by three hundred priests.

Asteria, daughter of Caeus, was carried away by Jupiter, who assumed the form of an eagle.

Astraea, daughter of Astraeus, king of Arcadia, or some say of Titan and Aurora, others Jupiter and Themis. She was mother of Nemesis. She was called Justice, of which virtue she was goddess.

Astyanax, son of Hector and Andromache. He was a child when the Greeks besieged Troy; when the city was taken his mother saved him in her arms from the flames. Euripides says he was slain by Menelaus.

Atalanta, daughter of Schoeneus, king of Scyros. According to some she was daughter of Jasus, or Jasius, and Clymene, but others say Menalion was her father. The oracle told her marriage would be fatal and she determined to live in celibacy. But her beauty gained her many suitors. To free herself from their attentions she proposed to run a race with them. As she was a very swift runner her suitors were defeated. She had said she would marry the winner, but all the defeated should be slain. Hippomenes, son of Marcareus, proposed himself as a suitor and Venus gave him three golden apples from the garden of the Hesperides, and with these concealed he entered the lists to race against Atalanta. As he ran he dropped the apples, which she stopped to pick up, thus allowing Hippomenes to arrive first at the goal and gain his bride. Afterwards they were both changed into lions by Cybele, for profaning her temple.

Ate, daughter of Jupiter, goddess of revenge and all evil. She raised such discord among the gods that Jupiter banished her from heaven to earth where she incited mankind to evil thoughts and actions.

Athanasius, Bishop of Alexandria, renowned for his determined opposition to Arius and his doctrines. He died A.D. 373, after filling the archiepiscopal chair for forty-seven years. The so-called Athanasian creed is of doubtful origin.

Athena, name obtained by Minerva as the tutelary goddess of Athens.

Atlas, one of the Titans, son of Iapetus and Clymene. He married Pleione, daughter of Oceanus, or some say Hesperis. He had seven daughters who were called Atlantides or Pleiades. He was a great astronomer and is depicted with the globe on his shoulders, his name meaning great labour. For his inhospitality to Perseus that king changed him into the mountain which bears his name. A chain of mountains in Africa is named after him, and so is the Atlantic Ocean. By another wife, Aethra, he had seven more daughters called Hyades. Both the Pleiades and Hyades are constellations.

Atreus, son of Pelops and Hippodamia, was king of Mycenae. His brother Chrysippus was illegitimate, and Hippodamia wished to get rid of him, and urged Atreus, and another of her sons, Thyestes, to murder him, which on their refusal she did herself. Atreus retired to the court of Eurystheus, king of Argos, and succeeded him. He is said to have hated Thyestes to the extent of killing and roasting his nephews, and inviting their father to a feast, which Thyestes thought was a sign of reconciliation, but he was victim of Atreus' cruelty.

Atticus, T. Pomponius, renowned Roman knight, to whom Cicero wrote a number of letters, containing the history of the age. He retired to Athens, where he endeared himself to the citizens, who erected statues to him in commemoration of his virtues. He died B.C. 32 aged seventy-seven.

Attila, renowned king of the Huns who invaded the Roman Empire in the time of Valentinian with an army of half a million. He laid waste the provinces and marched on Rome, but withdrew on being paid a vast sum. He called himself the Scourge of God. He died A.D. 453, of an effusion of blood, on his marriage night.

Atys, son of Croesus, was born dumb, but when fighting he saw a soldier about to kill the king. He gained speech, and shouted, "Save the king!"

Atys, youth beloved by Aurora, who was slain by her father, but Ovid says he was later turned into a pine-tree.

Augaeas, king of Elis, and owner of the stable cleaned by Hercules after three thousand oxen had lived in it for thirty years. It was cleansed by turning the river Alpheus through it. Augaeas promised to give Hercules a tenth part of his cattle for his trouble, but, neglecting to keep his promise, Hercules slew him.

Augury, the means adopted by the Romans of forming a judgment of futurity by the flight of birds; the officiating priest was called an augur.

Augustus, Octavianus Caesar, Roman Emperor, son of Octavius, a senator, and Accia, sister to Julius Caesar. He shared the triumvirate with Antony and Lepidus, and defeated the armies of Brutus and Cassius at Philippi. Octavia, sister of Augustus, married Antony after the death of his wife Fulvia. Octavia was slighted for the charms of Cleopatra, which angered Augustus, who took up arms to avenge the wrongs of his sister. At the great battle of Actium in B.C. 31, the forces of Antony and Cleopatra were defeated.

Aurelianus, Roman Emperor. He was cruel and austere in the execution of laws and treatment of his soldiers. He was a famous soldier, and his expedition against Zenobia, queen of Palmyra, gained him great honours. He is said himself to have killed eight hundred men in various battles. He was assassinated near Byzantium, A.D. 275.

Aurelius, M. Antoninus, surnamed "the Philosopher," possessed all the virtues required in a prince. He raised his brother, L. Verus, to the imperial dignity, but his dissipation was as conspicuous as the moderation of the philosopher. During their reign the Quadi, Parthians, and Marcomanni were defeated. Verus died of apoplexy, and Antoninus survived him eight years, dying at the age of sixty-one after reigning nineteen years and ten days.

Aurora, daughter of Hyperion and Thia or Thea. She is represented by the poets as sitting in a chariot and opening with her fingers the gates of the east, pouring dew on the earth, and making flowers grow. She was called Eos by the Greeks.

Auster, the south wind, a son of Jupiter.

Avernus, poisonous lake, referred to by poets as being at the entrance to the infernal regions, but really a lake in Campania, Italy.

Averruncus Deus, a Roman god who could divert people from evildoing.

Axe, see Daedalus.

B

Baal, a god of the Phoenicians.

Baal-Peor, a Moabitish god, associated with licentiousness and obscenity. The modern name is Belphegor.

Babes, see Rumina Dea.

Bacchantes, priestesses of Bacchus.

Bacchus, the god of wine, son of Jupiter and Semele. He is said to have married Ariadne, daughter of Minos, king of Crete, after she was deserted by Theseus. His most distinguished offspring was Hymen, god of marriage. Bacchus is sometimes called Dionysius, Biformis, Brisoeus, Iacchus, Lenaeus, Lyceus, Liber, and Liber Pater, the symbol of liberty. He is usually represented as crowned with vine and ivy leaves. In his left hand a thyrsus, a kind of javelin, having a fir cone for the head, and being encircled with ivy or vine. His chariot is drawn by lions, tigers, or panthers.

Balios, famous horse given by Neptune to Peleus as a nuptial gift, and later given to Achilles.

Barker, see Anubis.

Bassarides, priestesses of Bacchus were sometimes so called.

Battle, see Valhalla.

Bear, see Calisto.

Beauty, see Venus.

Bees, see Mellona.

Belisama, goddess of the Gauls. The name means Queen of Heaven.

Belisarius, famous general in the reign of Justinian, emperor of Constantinople, who renewed the victories which had rendered the first Romans so distinguished. He died B.C. 565.

Bellerophon, son of Glaucus, king of Ephyre, and Eurymede.

He was first called Hipponous. He was sent by Iobates, king of Lycia, to conquer the monster Chimaera. Minerva aided him in the expedition, and with the help of the winged horse Pegasus he conquered the monster and returned victorious. After sending him on other dangerous missions, Iobates gave him his daughter and made him his successor.

Bellona, goddess of war, daughter of Phorcys and Ceto, called by the Greeks Enyo, and is often confounded with Minerva. She prepared the chariot of Mars when he went to war, and appeared in battles armed with a whip to animate the combatants.

Belus, ancient king of Babylon, about 1800 years before the age of Semiramis, was made a god after death, and worshipped by the Assyrians and Babylonians. He was thought to be son of Osiris of the Egyptians. The temple of Belus was the most ancient and magnificent in the world, and was said to have been originally the Tower of Babel.

Berecynthia, a name of Cybele, from a mountain where she was worshipped.

Berenice, daughter of Philadelphus, who married Antiochus, king of Syria, after he had divorced Laodice.

Berenice, mother of Agrippa, whose name appears in the history of the Jews as daughter-in-law of Herod the Great. Others of the same name are less well known.

Biformis, a name of Bacchus, because he was accounted both bearded and beardless.

Bion, philosopher of Scythia who was famous for poetry, music and philosophy. Another of the same name was a Greek poet of Smyrna who wrote pastorals. He was a friend of Moschus, who says that he died by poison about 300 B.C.

Blacksmith, see Brontes and Vulcan.

Blind, see Thanyris.

Blue eyes, see Glaukopis.

Boadicea, famous British queen who rebelled against the Romans and was defeated, on which she poisoned herself. Her cruel treatment by the Romans is the subject of an ode by Cowper.

Bona Dea, "the bountiful goddess," whose festival was celebrated by the Romans with great magnificence. See Ceres.

Bonus Eventus, god of good success, a rural divinity.

Boreas, the name of the north wind blowing from the Hyperborean Mountains. According to the poets, he was son of Astraeus and Aurora. He was passionately fond of Hyacinthus.

Boundaries, see Terminus.

Boxing, see Pollux.

Brahma, great Indian deity, represented with four heads looking to the four quarters of the globe.

Brennus, general of the Gallic Senones, who defeated the Romans, and marched into the city. The Romans fled to the Capitol, and left the city in the possession of the enemy. The Gauls climbed the Tarpeian rock in the night and would have taken the Capitol had not the Romans been awakened by the cackling of geese, on which they roused and repelled the enemy.

Briareus, famous giant, son of Coelus and Terra. He had a hundred hands and fifty heads and was called Aegeon.

Brisaeus, a name of Bacchus, referring to the use of grapes and honey.

Brontes, one of the Cyclops. He is the personification of a blacksmith.

Brutus, L. Junius, son of M. Junius and Tarquinia. When Lucretia killed herself, B.C. 509, in consequence of the cruelty of Tarquin, Brutus snatched the dagger from the wound and swore upon the bloody blade immortal hatred to the royal family, and made the people swear they would no longer submit to the kingly authority. His sons conspired to restore the Tarquins, and were tried and condemned before their father, who himself was present at their execution.

Brutus, Marcus Junius, father of Caesar's murderer, followed the party of Marius, and was conquered by Pompey, by whose orders he was put to death.

Brutus, Marcus Junius, the destroyer of Caesar, conspired with many illustrious citizens of Rome against Caesar, and stabbed him in Pompey's basilica. There was a great tumult following the murder but the conspirators fled to the Capitol, and by proclaiming freedom and liberty to the people, for a time secured tranquillity. Antony, however, soon obtained the popular ear, and the murderers fled. Brutus went to Greece where he gained many friends. He was soon pursued by Antony, who was accompanied by the young Octavius. The famous battle of Philippi ensued, in which Brutus and his friend Cassius, who commanded the left wing of the army, were totally defeated. Brutus fell on his own sword B.C. 42, and was honoured with a magnificent funeral by Antony. Plutarch says that Caesar's ghost appeared to Brutus in his tent before the battle of Philippi warning him of his approaching fall.

Bubona, goddess of herdsmen, one of the rural divinities.

Bucephalus, Alexander's horse. He was the only person that could mount him, and he always knelt for his master to bestride him.

Buddha, Vishnu of the Hindoos.

Byblis, a niece of Sol, mentioned by Ovid. She shed so many tears of unrequited love that she was turned into a fountain.

C

Cabiri, mysterious rites in connection with the worship of these deities were so obscene that most writers refer to them as secrets which it was unlawful to reveal.

Cacodaemon, Greek name for an evil spirit.

Cacus, a famous robber, son of Vulcan and Medusa, represented as a three-headed monster vomiting flames. He lived in a cave in Italy and his dwelling was hung with human bones. When Hercules returned from the conquest of Geryon, Cacus stole some of his beasts. Hercules therefore strangled him.

Cadmus, son of Agenor, king of Phoenicia, and Telephassa, or Agriope, was ordered by his father to seek his sister Europa, whom Jupiter had carried away. His search proving fruitless he consulted the oracle of Apollo, and was told to build a city where he saw a heifer stop in the grass, and call the country Boeotia. He found the heifer, and, needing water, he sent his companions to a neighbouring grove to fetch some. The water was guarded by a dragon who devoured them. Cadmus, tired of waiting, himself went to the place. He attacked the dragon and killed it, sowing its teeth in the ground, upon which a number of armed men rose from the earth. Cadmus threw a stone amongst them and they at once began to fight one another, and all but five were slain. These assisted him to build the city. Cadmus introduced the use of letters in Greece. His alphabet consisted of sixteen letters.

Caduceus, the rod carried by Mercury. It had two winged serpents entwined round the top end. It was reported to have the power of producing sleep. Milton refers to it as the opiate rod.

Caesar, surname given to the Julian family in Rome. After the name had been dignified in the person of Julius Caesar and his successors, it was given to the apparent heir of the empire. The first twelve emperors had the name. They reigned in the following order: Julius Caesar, Augustus, Tiberius, Caligula, Claudius, Nero, Galba, Otho, Vitellius, Vespasian, Titus, and Domitian. Suetonius wrote an exhaustive history of them. C. Julius Caesar, the first emperor, was son of L. Caesar and Aurelia, the daughter of Cotta. He was descended from Julus, son of Aeneas. His eloquence procured him friends at Rome, and his hospitality equally served to make him popular. He was appointed for five years over the Gauls. He enlarged the boundaries of the empire by conquest, and invaded Britain, which had hitherto been unknown to the Romans. The corrupt state of the Roman Senate, and the ambition of Caesar and Pompey, caused a civil war. Neither of these celebrated Romans would endure a superior, and the smallest matters were grounds for quarrels. By the influence of Pompey a decree was passed to strip Caesar of his power. Antony, as tribune, opposed this, and went to Caesar's camp with the news. So Caesar crossed the Rubicon, which was the boundary of his province. This made it a declaration of war, and Caesar entered Italy with his army. Pompey left Rome for Dyrrachium, and Caesar soon entered Rome. He then went to Spain, conquering the partisans of Pompey, and on his return was declared dictator and later consul. The hostile generals met in the plains of Pharsalia, and a great battle took place, B.C. 48. Pompey was defeated and fled to Egypt where he was slain. But Caesar's glory was to end. Enemies had sprung up around him, and a conspiracy of many influential Romans formed against him. Brutus, his intimate friend, took a leading part and assassinated him in the senate house in the Ides of March, B.C. 44, when he was fifty-six years old. He wrote his Commentaries on the Gallic Wars when the battles were fought, his work having purity of style. It was after his conquest of Pharnaces, king of Pontus, that he used the words, "Veni, vidi, vici." In Shakespeare's "Julius Caesar" he is assassinated uttering his last words, "Et tu Brute! Then fall Caesar."

Caligula, Roman emperor, son of Germanicus by Agrippina. He was proud, wanton, and cruel, and pleased when disasters befell his people, often expressing a wish that the Romans had but one head that he might have the pleasure of striking it off. He made a favourite horse consul and adorned it with costly trappings and ornaments. He was murdered, A.D. 41, aged twenty-nine, after reigning three years and ten months.

Calisto, an Arcadian nymph, turned into a she-bear by Jupiter. She was hunted by her son Arcas, who would have killed her had not Jupiter turned him into a he-bear. The nymph and her son form the constellations known as the Great and Little Bear.

Calliope, Muse presiding over epic poetry and rhetoric. She is usually depicted using a stylus and wax tablets.

Calpe, one of the Pillars of Hercules.

Calypso, one of the Oceanides, or daughters of Atlas, some say. When Ulysses was shipwrecked on her coasts she received him hospitably, and offered him immortality if he would remain as her husband. This he refused to do and after seven years he was permitted to depart from the island where Calypso reigned.

Cama, Indian god of love and marriage.

Cambyses, king of Persia, son of Cyrus the Great. He conquered Egypt, and was so disgusted with the superstition of the Egyptians that he killed their god Apis and plundered their temples.

Camillus, a name of Mercury, from his office as minister to the gods.

Camillus, L. Furius, renowned Roman, known as a second Romulus from his services to the country. He was exiled for distributing the spoils of Veii. During his banishment Rome was besieged by the Gauls under Brennus. He went to the relief of his country and was elected dictator. He rid Rome of the enemy. He died B.C. 365.

Campus Martius, a large plain near Rome where the youth were exercised in athletics and were taught to throw the discus, javelin, etc.

Canache, name of one of Actaeon's hounds.

Cannae, village of Apuleia, where Hannibal defeated the Roman consuls Aemylius and Varro, B.C. 216.

Canopus, Egyptian god of water, the conqueror of fire.

Capis, or Capula, a cup with ears used for drinking the health of the gods.

Capitolinum, renowned temple and citadel at Rome on the Tarpeian rock.

Capitolinus, a name of Jupiter, from the Capitoline Hill, on top of which stood his temple.

Capripedes, Pan, the Egipans, the Satyrs, and Fauns, so named on account of their goats' feet.

Caprotina, a name of Juno.

Caracalla, son of Septimus Severus, Roman emperor. He was notorious for his cruelties, having killed his brother Geta in his mother's arms and endeavoured to destroy the works of Aristotle. After a life of vice he was assassinated A.D. 217, aged forty-three.

Caractacus, king of the Britons, who was taken prisoner to Rome.

Carthago, Carthage, a city of Africa, and rival of Rome, mistress of Spain, Sicily, and Sardinia. The date of its foundation is unknown but it was most likely built by Dido about 870 years B.C., or according to some, 72 or 73 years before the foundation of Rome. It reached its highest glory in the time of Hamilcar and Hannibal.

Cassander, son of Antipater, master of Macedonia after his father's death. He reigned eighteen years.

Cassandra, daughter of Priam and Hecuba, was loved by Apollo who promised to grant her dearest wish. She obtained the power of seeing into the future. Some say she received the gift of prophecy, with her brother Helenus, by being placed as a child one night in Apollo's temple. Serpents were discovered wreathed round their bodies licking their ears, which gave them the power to see into futurity. She was allotted to Agamemnon in the division of the spoils of Troy, and was slain by Clytemnestra, wife of Agamemnon.

Cassiopeia, Ethiopian queen who set her beauty in comparison with Nereides, who chained her to a rock and left her to be devoured by a sea-monster. She was delivered by Perseus.

Cassius, C., Roman famous for being first quaestor to Crassus in his expedition against Parthia. He married Junia, sister of Brutus, and joined Brutus in the conspiracy to assassinate Caesar. Later he returned to Philippi with Brutus, commanding one wing of the army in the famous battle fought there. On the defeat of his forces he ordered a freedman to kill him, and he perished by the sword which inflicted the wound on Caesar. Brutus called him "the last of all the Romans."

Castalia, one of the fountains in Mt. Parnassus, sacred to the Muses.

Castalides, a name of the Muses, from the fountain Castalia.

Castor and Pollux, twin sons of Jupiter and Leda. Mercury carried them to Pallena, where they were educated. When they reached manhood they embarked with Jason in quest of the Golden Fleece. Pollux defeated and slew Amycus in the combat of the Cestus, and was considered to be the god and patron of boxing and wrestling. Castor distinguished himself in the management of horses.

Catilina, L. Sergius, a renowned Roman who squandered his fortune and then plotted the ruin of his country and conspired with others as dissolute as himself to extirpate the senate, plunder the treasury, and set Rome on fire. This plot, known as the Catiline conspiracy, was unsuccessful. Its history is recorded by Sallust. Catilina died in battle, B.C. 63.

Cato, Marcus, great-grandson of the censor Cato. His early virtues seemed to promise that he would be great. He was austere in his morals and a strict follower of the tenets of the Stoics. His fondness for candour was so great that his veracity was proverbial. In the Catilinian conspiracy he supported Cicero, and was the chief cause of the capital punishment inflicted on some of the conspirators. He stabbed himself after reading Plato's treatise on the immortality of the soul, B.C. 46 when fifty-nine years old.

Catullus, C. or Q. Valerius, poet of Verona who wrote with luxuriant imagination. He was acquainted with the most distinguished people of his age. He directed his satire against Caesar, whose only revenge was to invite him to a sumptuous feast.

Cauther, Lake of Paradise in Mohammedan mythology, whose waters are sweet as honey, cold as snow, and clear as crystal. Any believer tasting thereof thirsts no more.

Celeno, one of the Harpies, progenitor of Zephyrus, the west wind.

Celsus, physician in the age of Tiberius, who wrote eight books on medicine, and, in addition, treatises on agriculture, rhetoric, and military affairs.

Centauri, a people of Thessaly, half men and half horses. They were the offspring of Centaurus and Stilbia.

Centumviri, members of a court of justice at Rome. Originally 105 in number they were known as Centumvirs, and this name they retained when increased to 180.

Cephalus, married Procris, whom he accidentally killed by shooting while she was secretly watching him, he thinking she was a wild beast. Cephalus was the type of constancy.

Ceraunius, a Greek name of Jupiter, meaning The Fulminator, from his thunderbolts.

Cerberus, a dog of Pluto. Hesiod says he had fifty heads, but others, only three. He was placed at the entrance to the infernal regions to prevent the living from entering, and the inhabitants from escaping.

Ceremonies, see Themis.

Ceres, daughter of Saturn and Vesta, was goddess of corn and harvests. She taught Triptolemus how to grow corn and sent him to teach the inhabitants of the earth. She was known by the names of Magna Dea, Bona Dea, Alma Mammosa, and Thesmorphonis. Ceres was mother of Proserpina, who was carried away by Pluto whilst gathering flowers.

Cestus, the girdle of Venus, which excited irresistible love.

Chaeronea, city of Boeotia celebrated for the great battle fought there in which the Athenians were defeated B.C. 447, and for Philip's victory there over the confederate armies of the Thebans and Athenians, B.C. 338. It was the birthplace of Plutarch.

Chaos, allegorically represented the confused mass of matter supposed to have existed before the creation, out of which the world was formed.

Charon, son of Nox and Erebus. He was the ferryman who conveyed the spirits of the dead over the rivers Acheron and Styx to the Elysian Fields. "Charon's toll" was a coin put into the hands of the dead with which to pay the ferryman.

Charybdis, dangerous whirlpool on the coast of Sicily. Personified it was supposed to have been a woman who plundered travellers, but was at last killed by Hercules. Scylla and Charybdis are generally spoken of together to represent alternative dangers.

Chemos, Moabitish god of war.

Cheops, king of Egypt, after Rhampsinitus, famous for building pyramids.

Children, see Nundina.

Chimaera, a wild illusion, personified in the monster slain by Bellerophon. It had the head and breast of a lion, the body of a goat, and the tail of a serpent. It used to vomit fire.

Chiron, a Centaur, half man and half horse. He was famous for music, medicine, and shooting, and taught mankind the use of plants and medicinal herbs. He was tutor to Achilles. Jupiter placed him among the stars, where he appears as Saggitarius, the Archer.

Chloris, Greek name of Flora, the goddess of flowers.

Chou, Egyptian god corresponding to the Roman Hercules.

Chronos, time, the Grecian name of Saturn.

Chrysostom, Bishop of Constantinople, died in A.D. 407. He was a great disciplinarian, making many enemies by severely lashing the vices of his day.

Cicero, M. T., son of a Roman knight, born at Arpinum and descended from the ancient kings of the Sabines. He displayed great ability in youth, and was taught philosophy by Philo, and law by Mutius Scaevola. He applied himself with great diligence to the study of oratory and was distinguished above all speakers in the Roman Forum. He signalised himself in opposing Catilina, whom he publicly accused of treason against the state, and whom he drove from the city. After a number of vicissitudes he was assassinated, B.C. 43, aged sixty-three.

Cillaros, see Cyllaros.

Cincinnatus, L. Q., renowned Roman, who was informed as he ploughed in the fields that the senate had chosen him to be dictator. Upon this he left the plough and went to the field of battle, where his countrymen were opposed by the Volsci and Aequi. He conquered the enemy and entered Rome in triumph.

Circe, daughter of Sol and Perseis, renowned for her knowledge of magic and poisonous herbs. She was carried by her father to an island called Aeaea. Ulysses on his return from the Trojan war visited her coasts, and his companions were changed, by her potions, into swine. Ulysses, who was fortified against enchantments by an herb he had received from Mercury, demanded of Circe the restoration of his companions to their former shape. She complied with his wishes, and eventually permitted him to depart from her island.

Cisseta, one of Actaeon's hounds.

Citherides, name of the Muses, from Mt. Citheron.

Claudianus, celebrated poet, in the age of Honorius, who is considered by some to equal Virgil in the majestic character of his style.

Claudius, T. Drusus Nero, son of Drusus, became emperor of Rome after Caligula. He went to Britain and obtained a triumph from victories achieved by his generals. He allowed himself to be influenced by favourites whose avarice plundered the State and distracted the provinces. He was poisoned by Agrippina, who wished to raise her son Nero to the throne.

Cleopatra, queen of Egypt, daughter of Ptolemy Auletes, was celebrated for her beauty. Antony fell in love with her and married her, forsaking Octavia, the sister of Augustus. He gave her the greatest part of the eastern provinces of the Roman Empire. This caused a rupture between Augustus and Antony; they met at the famous battle at Actium, when Cleopatra, by flying with sixty ships, ruined the battle for Antony, and he was defeated. Cleopatra killed herself by applying an asp to her breast.

Clio, one of the Muses. She presided over history.

Cloacina, goddess at Rome who presided over Cloacae, which were large receptacles for the filth of the whole city.

Clotho, youngest of the three Parcae, who were daughters of Jupiter and Themis. She presided over the moment of birth and held in her hand the distaff and spun the thread of life.

Clowns of Lycia, were changed into frogs by Latona for refusing to allow her to drink at one of their streamlets.

Cluacina, a name of Venus, given to her at the time of the reconciliation of the Romans and Sabines, which was ratified near a statue of the goddess.

Clytemnestra, daughter of Tyndarus, king of Sparta, and Leda, married Agamemnon, king of Argos, during whose absence at the Trojan war she misconducted herself with his cousin Aegysthus. On the return of Agamemnon Clytemnestra murdered him, as well as Cassandra, whom he had brought with him. After, Clytemnestra ascended the throne of Argos. In the meantime her son Orestes, after an absence of seven years, returned, determined to avenge the death of his father Agamemnon. When Aegysthus and Clytemnestra went to the temple of Apollo, Orestes, with his friend Pylades, killed them.

Clytia, or Clytie, daughter of Oceanus and Tethys, beloved of Apollo. She got herself changed into a sunflower, thus she is still turning towards Sol, one of Apollo's names.

Cneph, the creator of the universe in Egyptian mythology.

Cocles, P. Horatius, renowned Roman who opposed single-handed the army of Porsenna at the head of a bridge while his companions were cutting off communication with the other bank. When the bridge had been destroyed, Cocles, though wounded, leapt into the Tiber and swam across in his armour. For this heroism a statue was raised to him in the temple of Vulcan.

Cocytus, River of Lamentation, one of the five rivers of the infernal regions.

Codrus, last king of Athens, son of Melanthus. When Heraclidae made war against Athens, the oracle said victory would go to the nation whose king was killed in battle. The Heraclidae on hearing this ordered the life of Codrus to be spared, but the patriotic king disguised himself and engaged one of the enemy and was killed. The Athenians were victorious, and Codrus was regarded as saviour of his country.

Coeculus, son of Vulcan, and a violent robber.

Coelus, or Uranus, most ancient of the gods, supposed to be father of Saturn, Oceanus, and Hyperion.

Coena Saliaris, see Ancilia.

Colchis, or Colchos, country of Asia famous for the expedition of the Argonauts, and as being the birthplace of Medea.

Collatinus, L. Tarquinius, nephew of Tarquin the Proud. He married Lucretia. With Brutus he drove the Tarquins from Rome.

Collina, a rural deity, the goddess of hills.

Colossus, celebrated image at Rhodes, which was considered one of the seven wonders of the world.

Comedy, see Thalia.

Commodus, L. Aurelius Antoninus, son of M. Antoninus, succeeded his father in the Roman Empire. He was cruel and licentious. Desiring to be likened to Hercules, he wore a lion's skin about his shoulders and carried a knotted club. He fought with the gladiators, and boasted of his skill in killing wild beasts. He was strangled by a wrestler in A.D. 192, aged 31.

Comus, the god of revelry, feasting and nocturnal amusements. He is pictured as a drunken young man with a torch.

Concord, the symbol of Concord was two right hands joined, and a pomegranate.

Concordia, goddess of peace and concord at Rome, to whom Camillus raised a temple in the Capitol.

Confucius, Chinese philosopher, as much honoured among his countrymen as if he had been a king. He died about B.C. 499.

Conon, son of Timotheus, and a famous general of Athens. He governed all the islands of the Athenians, and was defeated by Lysander in a naval engagement. He gained a victory over the Spartans, near Cnidos, when Pisander, the enemy's admiral, was killed. He died B.C. 393 in prison.

Constancy, see Cephalus.

Constantia, granddaughter of Constantine the Great, who married the emperor Gratian.

Constantinus, surnamed the Great from the greatness of his exploits. He was son of Constantius. It is said that as he was going to fight against Maxentius, a rival of his, he saw a cross in the sky with the inscription, "In hoc signo vinces." Thus he became a convert to Christianity, and adopted the cross as his standard. He founded a city where old Byzantium formerly stood, calling it Constantinopolis. There he kept court, and made it rival Rome in population and magnificence. He reigned thirty-one years, dying in A.D. 337.

Constantius Chlorus, son of Eutropius, and father of Constantine the Great, made victories in Germany and Britain. He was a colleague of Galerius after the abdication of Dioclesian. He was reputed to be benevolent, brave, and humane, and died A.D. 306.

Consualia, games sacred to Neptune.

Consul, Roman magistrate with regal authority for one year. Two consuls were chosen annually in the Campus Martius. The first two were L. Jun. Brutus and L. Tarquinius Collatinus.

Consus, name of Neptune as god of counsel.

Corinna, daughter of Archelodorus. She is said to have won a poetical prize five times in competition with Pindar. She was born at Thebes.

Coriolanus, surname of C. Martius from his victory over Corioli. In spite of his military prowess and his services to his country he was refused a consulship and banished to Volsci where he was received by Tullus Aufidius. Coriolanus advised him to make war against Rome and marched with the Volsci as their general. His approach alarming the Romans they sent his wife and mother to appease his resentment against his countrymen; they succeeded with difficulty. Shakespeare in his tragedy, "Coriolanus," ends the play with the assassination of the hero by Tullus Aufidius.

Corn, see Ceres.

Cornelia, daughter of Scipio Africanus, famous for learning and virtue. She was mother of Gracchi, Tiberius, and Caius Gracchus.

Coronis, consort of Apollo and mother of Aesculapius. Another

Coronis was daughter of a king of Phocis, who was changed by Athena into a crow.

Corybantes, priests of Cybele so called from their habit of striking themselves in their dances.

Corydon, silly love-sick swain mentioned by Virgil.

Corythaix, name of Mars, meaning Shaker of the Helmet.

Cotytto, Athenian goddess of immodesty.

Counsel, see Consus.

Crassus, M. Licinius, famous Roman who by educating slaves and selling them became wealthy. He was made consul with Pompey, and later censor, and formed one of the first triumvirate with Pompey and Caesar. He left Rome with a view to enlarging his possessions, crossed the Euphrates and tried to make himself master of Parthia. He was met by Surena the Parthian general and in the ensuing engagement 20,000 Romans were killed and 10,000 made prisoner. Crassus surrendered and was put to death B.C. 53.

Creditors, see Jani.

Creon, king of Thebes whose kingdom was ravished by the Sphinx. He offered his crown to any who could explain the enigmas proposed by the Sphinx. Oedipus solved the riddles and ascended the throne.

Creon, king of Corinth, son of Sisyphus. He promised his daughter Glauce to Jason who had forsaken Medea, who, to revenge herself sent Glauce a poisoned dress. On assuming it Glauce was seized with sudden pain. Her body ignited and she died in great agony, while the house in which she was also was consumed. Creon and his family shared Glauce's fate.

Croesus, fifth and last of the Mermnadae. He was son of Alyattes and was king of Lydia. Considered the richest man in the world, his court was a centre of learning, while Aesop and other intellectuals lived under his patronage. Subject of the proverb, "As rich as Croesus."

Crow, see Coronis.

Cultivated land, see Sylvester.

Cup-bearer, see Ganymede.

Cupido, god of love, son of Jupiter and Venus, is depicted as a naked, winged infant, armed with bow and arrows. On ornaments he is generally represented amusing himself in some childish diversion. He could, in common with the rest of the gods, assume different forms. In the Aeneid he is represented as putting on the form of Ascanius, at the request of his mother, and going to Dido's court where he inspired the queen with love.

Curtius, M., a Roman devoted to the service of his country, lived about 360 B.C. He leapt on horseback fully armed, into a huge gap in the earth at the command of the oracle.

Cuvera, Indian god of wealth corresponding to the Greek Plutus.

Cybele, goddess, daughter of Coelus and Terra and wife of Saturn. She was mother of the gods and is variously referred to as Ceres, Rhea, Ops, Vesta, etc. According to Diodorus she was daughter of a Lydian prince. On her birth she was exposed on a mountain where she was nurtured by the wild beasts. She took her name from the mountain on which she was preserved. She is depicted as riding in a chariot drawn by lions. She holds a sceptre in one hand and a key in the other. On her head is a castellated crown, denoting that she was the first protector of castles and walls with towers.

Cyclopes, race of men of gigantic stature having a single eye in the middle of the forehead. They were the supposed sons of Coelus and Terra. They laboured for Vulcan, who made Jove's thunderbolts. Hesiod says they were three in number, Arges, Brontes, and Steropes.

Cygnus, bosom friend of Phaeton who died of grief on the death of his friend and was changed into a swan.

Cyllaros, one of Castor's horses, jet-black with white legs and tail. See Cillaros.

Cyllo, one of Actaeon's hounds which was lame.

Cyllopotes, another of Actaeon's hounds.

Cynosure, one of Jupiter's nurses turned by him into a constellation.

Cyparissus, boy of whom Apollo was fond. When he died he was changed, at Apollo's intercession, into a cypress tree, typifying mourning.

Cypria, a name of Venus given because she was worshipped in Cypress.

Cyrus, king of Persia, son of Cambyses and Mandanae, daughter of Astyages, king of Media. Xenophon, in his life, describes him as a brave and virtuous prince and often puts into his mouth the sayings of Socrates.

Cyrus the Younger was son of Darius Nothus and brother of Artaxerxes, the latter ascending the throne on the death of Nothus. Cyrus commanded Lydia and the sea-coasts where he incited rebellion and raised troops under various pretences. He took the field with 100,000 Barbarians and 13,000 Greeks commanded by Clearchus. Artaxerxes met him with 900,000 men near Cunaxa. Cyrus was killed in the battle B.C. 401.

Cythera, a name of Venus from the island to which she was wafted in the shell.

D

Dactyli, priests of Cybele, so named because, like the fingers, they were ten in number.

Daedalus, most ingenious Athenian artist. He invented the wedge, axe, level, gimlet and was first to make use of sails. He produced the famous labyrinth for Minos, king of Crete, but incurring his displeasure was himself confined therein. He made wings with feathers and wax, fitting them to his body and to that of his son Icarus who was confined with him. They rose in the air but the sun melted the wax on the wings of Icarus who fell into the ocean which has since been called the Icarian Sea. Daedalus landed at Cumae where he built a temple to Apollo.

Dagon, god of the Philistines, was half man and half fish. Milton describes him as "upward man and downward fish."

Dahak, the Persian devil.

Daityas, devils or evil gods of Hindoo mythology.

Danae, daughter of Acrisius, king of Argos, and Eurydice. She had a son by Jupiter. Acrisius set Danae and her child adrift on the open sea. The winds drove them to the island of Seriphus where they were saved by fishermen who took them to Polydectes, the king of Seriphus, whose brother Dictys educated the child, who was named Perseus, and kindly treated the mother.

Danaides, the fifty daughters of Danaus, king of Argos; they married the fifty sons of their uncle Aegyptus. Danaus had been warned by the oracle that he would be killed by a son-in-law, so he made his daughters promise to kill their husbands immediately after marriage. All fulfilled their father's will except Hypermnestra, who spared her husband Lynceus. For their crime they were condemned to endeavour to draw water forever using vessels without bottoms.

Danaus, king of Argos, see above.

Dancing, see Terpsichore.

Daphne, a daughter of the River Peneus, or of the Ladon, and Terra. Apollo courted her but she fled from him and, at her own request, was turned into a laurel. She was goddess of the earth.

Dardanus, son of Jupiter, who killed his brother Jasius to gain the kingdom of Etruria. He built the city of Dardania, and was accounted the founder of Troy.

Darius, a noble satrap of Persia, son of Hystaspes, who usurped the crown of Persia after the death of Cambyses. He was twenty-nine when he ascended the throne and soon distinguished himself by military exploits. He besieged Babylon and it fell after twenty months. He died B.C. 485.

Darius, second king of Persia by that name; he ascended the throne soon after the murder of Xerxes. He was successful in many wars aided by his son Cyrus the Younger and his generals. He reigned nineteen years and died B.C. 404.

Darius, third king of Persia of that name who had to take the field against Alexander, who invaded Persia. Darius met him with an enormous army better known for luxuriant living than military courage. The Persians were easily defeated near Granicus and another battle followed near Issus where the Persians were again beaten. Darius escaping assembled another great army. The decisive battle was fought at Arbela, Alexander being once more victorious. After the battle Darius was found in his chariot wounded and dying, B.C. 331.

Dead-toll, see Charon.

Death, see Nox.

Deceiver, see Apaturia.

Deianira, daughter of Oeneus, king of Aetolia. Her beauty attracted many suitors and her father promised her to him who should excel in a competition of strength. Hercules obtained the prize and married Deianira.

Delius, a name of Apollo from the island on which he was born.

Delphi, a town of Phocis at the southwest side of Mt. Parnassus, famous for a temple of Apollo, and for a celebrated oracle. See Delphos.

Demetrius, son of Antigonus and Stratonice, surnamed Poliorcetes (destroyer of cities). At twenty-two years of age his father sent him against Ptolemy, who had invaded Syria. He was defeated at Gaza, but later obtained a victory. Most of his life was spent in warfare with varying success. He was fond of dissipation when in dissolute society. He died B.C. 286.

Demetrius, surnamed Soter, king of Syria. His father gave him as a hostage to the Romans. After his father's (Seleucus Philopator) death, Antiochus Epiphanes usurped the throne of Syria, and was succeeded by Antiochus Eupator. Demetrius procured his liberty, and established himself on the throne, causing Eupator to be put to death.

Demetrius, son of Soter, whom he succeeded after driving Alexander Bala, a usurper, from the throne. Demetrius gave himself to luxury and allowed his kingdom to be governed by his favourites, so becoming unpopular with his subjects. He was killed by the governor of Tyre, where he had fled for protection.

Demetrius Phalereus, disciple of Theophrastus, who gained such influence over the Athenians by his eloquence and purity of manners, that he was elected decennial archon, B.C. 317. He improved the city, and made himself popular by his munificence. His enemies plotted against him, and he was forced to flee to the court of Ptolemy Lagos. He ended his life by allowing an asp to bite him, B.C. 284. Several others of the same name were of less note.

Democritus, famous philosopher of Abdera, one of the disciples of Leucippus; he travelled in Europe, Asia, and Africa, in quest of knowledge, and returned in poverty. He engaged in continuous laughter at the follies of mankind for distracting themselves with care and anxiety in the short span of their lives. He told Darius, who was lamenting the loss of his wife, that he would raise her from the dead if he could find three persons who had lived without adversity, whose names he might engrave on the queen's monument. He taught his disciples that the soul died with the body. He died aged one hundred and nine, B.C. 361. He has been known as "the laughing philosopher."

Demogorgon, was the tyrant genius of the soil, the life and support of plants. He was represented as an old man covered with moss, and was supposed to reside underground. He is sometimes called the king of elves and fays.

Deucalion, son of Prometheus, who wed Pyrrha, daughter of Epimetheus. He reigned over part of Thessaly, and in his reign the earth was flooded by Jupiter as a punishment for the evil of mankind. Deucalion built a ship, thus saving himself and Pyrrha. After tossing on the waves nine days, the ship rested on Mt. Parnassus. The deluge of Deucalion is supposed to have occurred B.C. 1503.

Devil, see Dahak, Daityas, and Obambou.

Diana, goddess of hunting. According to Cicero there were three of the name, one a daughter of Jupiter and Proserpina, a daughter of Jupiter and Latona, and a daughter of Upis and Glauce. The second is the most famous, all mention of Diana by ancient writers referring to her. To shun the society of men she devoted herself to hunting, always accompanied by a band of young women, who, like herself, abjured marriage. She is depicted with a quiver and attended by dogs. Her most famous temple was at Ephesus, and was one of the seven wonders of the world.

Dictator, a magistrate at Rome invested with regal authority.

Dictynna, a Greek name for Diana as terrestrial goddess.

Dido, daughter of Belus, king of Tyre, who married Sicharbus or Sichaeus, her uncle, who was a priest of Hercules. Pygmalion killed him to obtain his wealth. Dido, disconsolate, set sail with a number of Tyrians in quest of a place in which to establish a settlement. A storm drove her ships on to the African coast and she bought from the people as much land as could be covered by a bull's hide cut into thongs. On this land she built a citadel and called it Byrsa, which was the beginning of a great city. Her subjects wished her to remarry but she refused. She erected a funeral pile, on which she climbed and stabbed herself to death. Virgil however relates that when Aeneas was wrecked on a neighbouring coast, Dido received him with every kindness and at last fell in love with him. Her love not being returned, she was so grieved that she stabbed herself. In "Facetiae Cantabrigienses," a tale is told of Professor Porson, who being one of a set party, the conversation turned on punning. Porson remarked that he could pun on any subject. A member of the party defied him to do so on the Latin gerunds, di, do dum, which he immediately proceeded to do in the following couplet:

"When Dido found Aeneas would not come,
She mourned in silence, and was Dido dumb."

Dies Pater, Jupiter, Father of the Day.

Dii Selecti, the second class of gods, consisting of Coelus, Saturn, Genius, Oreus, Sol, Bacchus, Terra, and Luna.

Dindymene, a name of Cybele from a mountain where she was worshipped.

Diocletianus, Caius Valerius Jovius, famous Roman emperor, of obscure family, born in Dalmatia. He joined the army and attained the rank of general by sheer merit and at last became emperor. Though naturally unpolished he was the patron of learning and genius. He cruelly persecuted the Christians of his day. He reigned in great prosperity for twenty-one years and abdicated A.D. 304. He died A.D. 313 at the age of sixty-eight.

Diodorus, Siculus, famous historian. He wrote forty books on Egypt, Persia, Syria, Media, Greece, Rome, and Carthage. Fifteen and a few fragments remain.

Diogenes, famous cynic philosopher of Sinope, banished for uttering spurious coinage. He fled to Athens where he became the disciple of Antisthenes, who led the Cynics. He adopted their form of dress and walked about with a tub on his head, which served as his lodging. His singularity and great contempt for riches gained him a reputation. Alexander the Great visited him and asked if there was anything in which he could oblige him. "Get out of my sunshine," said the Cynic. Such independence pleased Alexander, and he said, "Were I not Alexander, I would wish to be Diogenes." Once he was sold as a slave, and his magnanimity so pleased his master, that he made him tutor of his children, and guardian of his lands. His life does not bear strict examination. While boasting of his poverty, he was so arrogant that his virtues arose from pride and vanity, not wisdom or philosophy. He died B.C. 324 aged ninety-six.

Diomedes, son of Tydeus and Deiphyle, was king of Aetolia, and one of the bravest Grecian chiefs in the Trojan war. He often engaged Hector and Aeneas and gained much military glory.

Diomedes, a tyrant of Thrace, who fed his mares with the flesh of his guests. He was overcome by Hercules, who gave him to his own horses to be devoured.

Dion, a Syracusan, son of Hipparina; he was related to Dionysius the First who became his adviser, and at whose court he gained great popularity. He was murdered by one of his own friends, B.C. 354. His death was lamented by the Syracusans who raised a memorial to him. When Dionysius the Second became king he banished Dion, who collected troops, and in three days made himself master of Syracuse.

Dione, a poetic name of Venus.

Dionysia, festivals in honour of Bacchus.

Dionysius, a name of Bacchus, from his father Jupiter (Dios), or from his nurses, the nymphs called Nysae.

Dionysius of Halicarnassus, historian who left his country and came to Rome to study all the authors who had written Roman history. His work on Roman antiquities, consisting of twenty volumes, engaged him for twenty-four years.

Dioscuri, Castor and Pollux, sons of Jupiter.

Dirae, a name of the Furies.

Dirce, woman whom Lycus, king of Thebes, married after his divorce from Antiope. Amphion and Zethus, sons of Antiope, tied Dirce to the tail of a wild bull by which she was dragged over rocks and precipices until the gods pitied her and changed her into a fountain. Antiope's sons had punished her for her cruelties to their father.

Dis, a name of Pluto, god of hell, signifying riches.

Discord, see Ate.

Discordia, malevolent deity, daughter of Nox, and sister to Nemesis, the Parcae, and Death. She was banished from heaven by Jupiter for sowing dissension amongst the gods. At the wedding of Peleus and Thetis, she threw an apple amongst the gods, inscribed "Detur Pulchriori," which was primary cause of the ruin of Troy, and of infinite misfortunes to the Greeks.

Diseases, see Pandora.

Distaff, see Pallas.

Dithrambus, a name of Bacchus.

Dodona, a celebrated oracle of Jupiter.

Dodonaeus, a name of Jupiter, from the city of Dodona.

Dog, see Lares.

Dolabella, P. Corn., Roman who married the daughter of Cicero. During the civil wars he espoused the cause of Caesar, whom he accompanied at the famous battles of Pharsalia and Munda.

Dolabra, knife used by the priests when cutting up sacrifices.

Dolphin, see Arion.

Domitianus, Titus Flavius, son of Vespasian and Flavia Domitilla, made himself emperor of Rome on the death of his brother Titus, whom he is said to have poisoned. His reign began hopefully, but Domitianus became cruel and self-indulgent. The latter part of his reign found him suspicious and remorseful. He was assassinated A.D. 96, aged forty-five.

Doorga, a Hindoo goddess.

Doris, daughter of Oceanus, and sister of Nereus, two sea deities. From these two sisters sprang several tribes of water nymphs.

Doto, one of the Nereids or sea-nymphs.

Draco, celebrated lawgiver at Athens. He produced a code of laws, B.C. 623, so severe that they were said to be written in letters of blood. The term "draconic" is derived from this source and is applied to punishment of unusual severity.

Dragon, seven-headed, see Geryon.

Dreams, see Morpheus.

Drusus, son of Tiberius and Vipsania, famous for courage at Illyricum and Pannonia.

Drusus, M. Livius, famous Roman, who renewed the proposals bearing on the agrarian laws, which had proved fatal to the Gracchi.

Drusus, Nero Claudius, son of Tiberius Nero and Livia. He distinguished himself in wars in Germany and Gaul, being honoured with a triumph. Other Romans of the same name were less noted.

Dryades, nymphs that presided over the woods. Milk, oil, and honey were offered to them. Sometimes votaries sacrificed a goat to them.

Dumbness, see Atys.

Duumviri, two patricians at Rome, first appointed by Tarquin to keep the Sibylline books, which were reputed to contain the fate of the Roman Empire.

E

Eachus, son of Jupiter and Egina, one of the judges of the infernal regions, who was appointed to judge Europeans. See Aeacus.

Earth, see Antaeas.

Eblis, Mohammedan evil genius.

Echidna, woman having a serpent's tail. Reputed mother of Chimera, also of the many-headed dog Orthos, of the Hesperides, of the Colchian dragon, of the Sphinx, of Cerberus, of Scylla, of the Gorgons, of the Lernaean Hydra, of the vulture that gnawed away the liver of Prometheus, also the Nemean lion; indeed the mother of all adversity and tribulation.

Echnobas, one of Actaeon's hounds.

Echo, reputed daughter of Air and Tellus, was one of Juno's attendants. She fell in love with Narcissus but when he languished and died, she pined and also died, preserving nothing but her voice which repeats every sound reaching her. Another fable says she was partly deprived of speech by Juno, only being allowed to reply to questions.

Egeon, giant sea-god who aided the Titans against Jupiter.

Egeria, nymph of Aricia in Italy, where Diana was particularly worshipped. Egeria was courted by Numa, and according to Ovid, became his wife. At the death of Numa she became so disconsolate and wept so copiously that Diana changed her into a fountain.

Egil, the Vulcan of northern mythology.

Egipans, rural deities inhabiting forests and mountains: they were half man and half goat.

Egis, the shield of Minerva. It got its name by being covered with the skin of the goat Amalthaea, which nourished Jupiter. See Aegis.

Electra, daughter of Agamemnon, king of Argos. She persuaded her brother Orestes to avenge his father's death by slaying his mother Clytemnestra. Her history forms the subject of one of the greatest of Sophocles' tragedies.

Eleusinia, great festival observed by the Lacedaemonians, Cretans, and others, every four years, and by the Athenians, every five years, at Eleusis in Attica. Eumolpus introduced it B.C. 1356. It was most famous of all religious ceremonies in Greece. The term "Mysteries" is often applied to it. The expression "Eleusinian Mysteries" is proverbial when applied to anything inexplicable.

Elysium, the Elysian Fields, a place in the infernal regions, where according to the ancients, the souls of the righteous existed after death.

Empedocles, philosopher, poet, and historian of Agrigentum in Sicily, 444 B.C. He was a Pythagorean, and an ardent believer in the transmigration of souls.

Empyrean, The, the fifth heaven, the seat of the heathen deity.

Endymion, a shepherd son of Aethlius and Calyce, said to have required of Jupiter that he might be always young. Diana saw him sleeping on Mt. Latmos, and was so impressed by his beauty that she left heaven every night to visit him.

Ennius, ancient poet, born in Calabria, who attained Roman citizenship on account of his learning and genius.

Entertainment, see Comus.

Envy, see Furies.

Enyo, Grecian name of Bellona, goddess of war and cruelty.

Eos, Grecian name for Aurora.

Eous, one of the four horses that drew the chariot of Sol, the sun. (A Greek word meaning red.)

Epaminondas, famous Theban descended from the ancient kings of Boeotia. He defeated the Spartans at the battle of Leuctra about B.C. 370. He died in battle aged forty-eight.

Ephesus, city of Iona, famous for the temple of Diana, then considered as one of the seven wonders of the world.

Ephialtes, giant who lost his right eye in an encounter with Hercules, while his left eye was destroyed by Apollo.

Epictetus, Stoic philosopher of Hieropolis, once the slave of Epaphroditus, the freedman of Nero. He believed in the immortality of the soul.

Epicurus, famous philosopher, born in Attica of humble parents. At school he was distinguished for brilliance. He taught that the happiness of man consisted in pleasure, which arises from mental enjoyment, and sweets of virtue. He died B.C. 270 aged seventy-two.

Erato, one of the Muses, presiding over lyric poetry. She is depicted as crowned with roses and myrtle, holding a lyre.

Erebus, son of Chaos, one of the gods of the infernal regions. Poets often use the name to signify the infernal regions.

Ergatis, name given to Minerva, meaning work-woman, because she was supposed to have invented spinning and weaving.

Erictheus, fourth king of Athens, and son of Vulcan.

Erinnys, Greek name for the Furies, signifying disturber of the mind.

Erisichthon, defiled the groves of Ceres, and felled a sacred oak, being punished with perpetual hunger.

Eros, Greek god of love.

Erostratus, burnt the temple of Diana at Ephesus, thus hoping to make his name immortal.

Erycina, a name of Venus, from Mt. Eryx in Sicily.

Erythreos, Greek name of one of Sol's chariot horses.

Esculapius, see Aesculapius.

Eta, see Aeta.

Eteocles, king of Thebes, son of Oedipus and Jocasta. After his father's death he agreed with his brother Polynices that they should reign a year alternately. Eteocles reigned first and refused to resign. Polynices asked assistance from Adrastus, king of Argos, whose daughter he wed, and who placed an army at his disposal. Eteocles mustered his forces and several skirmishes ensued. It was decided later that the brothers should decide by single combat. They fought furiously and both were killed.

Ethon, chariot-horse of Sol, the name meaning hot.

Etna, volcanic mountain beneath which Virgil says the giant Typhon is buried and breathes forth flames.

Euclides, famous mathematician of Alexandria B.C. 300. He wrote fifteen books on the elements of mathematics. Ptolemy was one of his pupils.

Eudromos, name of one of Actaeon's hounds.

Eulalon, one of the names of Apollo.

Eumenes, Greek officer in Alexander's army. After the death of Alexander he conquered Paphlagonia and Cappadocia, and obtained the government till Antigonus made him retire. He was executed in prison by order of Antigonus.

Eumenides, name given to the Furies. They sprang from drops of blood which flowed from the wound which Coelus received from Saturn. Some writers state that they were daughters of the earth, and sprang from the blood of Saturn, while others make them daughters of Acheron and Night, or Pluto or Proserpine. They were generally supposed to be three in number—Tisiphone, Megara, and Alecto, but some writers add Nemesis.

Euphorbus, famous Trojan who wounded Patroclus, whom Hector killed. Menelaus slew Euphorbus.

Euphrates, river of Asia flowing through the centre of Babylon.

Euphrosyne, one of the three Graces.

Euripides, famous tragic poet born at Salamis. He studied elocution under Prodicus, ethics under Socrates, and philosophy under Anaxagoras. He wrote his tragedies in a lonely cave. He is said to have met his death by being torn to pieces by dogs, B.C. 407 aged seventy-eight. Twenty-five tragedies have been attributed to him, of which nineteen remain.

Europa, daughter of Agenor, king of Phoenicia, and Telaphassa. Her beauty drew Jupiter's attention to her, and he transformed himself into a bull in order to become possessed of her. He mingled with the herds of Agenor whilst Europa was picking flowers. She stroked the animal and mounted on his back. Jupiter crossed the sea with her to Crete where he resumed his proper form, and declared his love. She became mother of Minos, Sarpedon, and Rhadamanthus.

Eurus, the east wind, a son of Aeolus.

Euryale, one of the Gorgons, daughter of Phorcus and Ceto.

Eurydice, wife of the poet Orpheus. Fleeing from Aristaeus, who was enamoured of her, she was bitten by a serpent and died. Orpheus, disconsolate at her loss, descended to the infernal regions in search of her. By the sweetness of his lyre he obtained her restoration, provided he did not look back as he returned to earth. His eagerness to see her caused him to violate the conditions, thus losing Eurydice forever.

Eurydice, wife of Amyntas, king of Macedonia, who conspired against him but was prevented from killing him by Euryone. Their children were: Alexander, Perdiceas, Philip and Euryone.

Eurysthenes, son of Aristodemus, who lived in continuous dissension with Procles, his twin brother, while they jointly ruled Sparta. His descendants were called Eurysthenidae, and those of Procles, Proclidae.

Eurystheus, king of Argos and Mycenae, son of Sthenelus and Nicippe. Juno hastened his birth by two months that he might be born before Hercules, the son of Alcmena, as the younger of the two had been doomed by Jupiter to be subservient to the other. This natural right was cruelly exercised by Eurystheus, who was jealous of the fame of Hercules. To destroy him he imposed upon him the most dangerous enterprises, known as the Twelve Labours of Hercules, all of which he successfully accomplished.

Eurythion, a seven-headed dragon. See Geryon.

Eusebius, bishop of Caesarea, in favour with the Emperor Constantine. He took part in the doctrinal disputes of Arius and Athanasius. He wrote a renowned ecclesiastical history and other works.

Euterpe, one of the Muses, daughter of Jupiter and Mnemosyne. She presided over instrumental music. Her name signifies agreeable.

Eutropius, Roman historian in the age of Julian. He wrote an epitome of the history of Rome from the time of Romulus to the reign of the Emperor Valens.

Euvyhe, meaning "Well done, son." Jupiter so frequently addressed Bacchus in this way that it at last became one of his names.

Evening Star, see Hesperus.

Evil, see Cacodaemon.

Evils, see Pandora.

Eye, see Cyclopes and Glaukopis.

F

Fabii, noble, powerful family of Rome. They fought with the Veientes, and all were killed. One of tender age remained in Rome and from him descended the family which later became so distinguished.

Fabius, Maximus Rullianus, was first of the Fabii to win the name "Maximus." He was master of the horse, and his victory over the Samnites in that capacity nearly cost him his life. He was five times Consul, twice Dictator, and once Censor.

Fabius, Q. Maximus, famous Roman who was raised to the highest office of the state. In his first consulship he gained a victory over Liguria and the battle of Thrasymenus caused his election to the dictatorship. As dictator he opposed Hannibal, harassing him more by strategy than fighting. He died aged one hundred, after being consul five times. Others of the family were of less distinction, though their names appear in Roman history.

Fabricius, Caius, distinguished Roman who in his first consulship gained victories over the Samnites and Lucanians. He had a very extensive knowledge of military matters but was simple and unassuming in his mode of life.

Falernus, fertile mountain and plain of Campania, famous for wine. Falernian wine was esteemed by the Romans and the poets often allude to it.

Fame, was a poetical deity, depicted with wings and a trumpet. The Romans dedicated a temple to her.

Fate, see Nereus.

Fates, or Parcae, three daughters of Necessity. Clotho held the distaff, Lachesis turned the spindle, and Atropos cut the thread with the fatal shears.

Faun, rural deity, half man half goat. They were similar to the Satyrs. The fauns attended Pan, and the Satyrs Bacchus.

Fauni, rural deities depicted as having legs, ears, and feet of a goat, and the rest of the body human.

Favonius, wind favourable to vegetation. Zephyr, the west wind.

Fays, "The yellow-skirted fays fly after the night-steeds, leaving their moon-loved maze."—Milton.

Feasts, see Comus.

Febris, one of the evil deities, worshipped that she might do no harm.

Februus, name of Plato, from part of the funeral rites consisting of purifications.

Feronia, Roman goddess of orchards, and patroness of enfranchised slaves. Some writers have identified her with Juno.

Fertility, see Lupercus.

Festivals, see Thalia.

Fidelity, see Iolaus.

Fides, goddess of faith and honesty, who had a temple in the Capitol of Rome.

Fine Arts, see Minerva.

Fire, see Salamander, Vesta, and Vulcan.

Fisherman, see Glaucus.

Flaccus, consul who marched against Sylla and was assassinated.

Flaminius, T. Q., famous Roman trained in the art of war against Hannibal. He commanded Roman troops against Philip of Macedonia with success.

Flathinnis, Paradise of Celtic mythology.

Fleece, Golden, see Golden Fleece, Argonauts, and Jason.

Flies, see Muscarius.

Flocks, see Pales.

Flora, goddess of flowers and gardens, and was wife of Zephyrus. She enjoyed perpetual youth. She was the same as Chloris of the Greeks.

Floralia, licentious games in honour of the goddess Flora.

Flowers, see Flora, Cloris, Hortensis, and Zephyrus.

Flute, see Marsyas.

Fortuna, goddess of fortune. Servius Tullius erected a temple to her. She was supposed to bestow riches or poverty upon mankind and was reckoned one of the most potent of the ancient goddesses. She is depicted standing on a wheel, with her eyes bandaged, holding a cornucopia. Homer makes her daughter of Oceanus, but Pindar one of the Parcae.

Fraud, one of the evil deities, depicted as a goddess with a human face and a serpent's body, and in the end of her tail a scorpion's sting. She resided in the river Cocytus, nothing but her head ever being seen.

Freyja, Scandinavian Venus, goddess of love.

Freyr, Scandinavian god of fertility and peace. Patron god of Sweden and Iceland.

Friga, Saxon goddess of earthly enjoyments. The name of the day of the week Friday is derived from her. In Scandinavian mythology she is goddess of marriage.

Fro, Scandinavian god of tempests and winds.

Frogs, see Clowns of Lycia.

Fruits, see Ceres and Pomona.

Fulvia, wife of the tribune Clodius; an ambitious woman. Later she married Curio, and lastly Antony. Antony divorced her for Cleopatra. She attempted to avenge herself by persuading Augustus to take arms against Antony.

Funerals, see Libitina and Manes.

Furies, The, three daughters of Acheron and Nox. They were punishers of evildoers. They were named Tisiphone, Megaera, and Alecto, and were reputed to personify rage, slaughter, and envy.

Futurity, see Cassandra.

G

Gabriel, prince of fire and thunder in Jewish mythology.

Galataea, sea nymph, daughter of Nereus and Doris, loved by Polyphemus, the Cyclopes, whom she treated with disdain. She was in love with Acis, a shepherd of Sicily.

Galba, Servius Sulpicius, a Roman who rose to the great state offices, exercising his power with equity until he ascended the throne, when his virtues disappeared. He was assassinated in his seventy-third year.

Gallantes, mad men of Galli, q.v.

Galli, priests of Cybele who used to cut their arms with knives when sacrificing, and acted so much like mad men that demented people got the name of Gallantes.

Gallienus, Pub. Licinius, son of the Emperor Valerian, who reigned conjointly with his father for seven years, becoming sole emperor, A.D. 260. When young he led an expedition against the Germans and Sarmatae. As emperor he gave himself to pleasure and vice. He was assassinated A.D. 268 aged fifty.

Gallus, Cornelius, famous Roman knight and poet. He was greatly attached to his slave Lycoris (or Cytheris), whose beauty he extolled in his poetry.

Ganesa, the Indian Mercury, god of wisdom and prudence.

Ganga, one of three Indian river goddesses.

Ganymedes, beautiful youth of Phrygia, son of Tros, king of Troy. He was taken to heaven by Jupiter whilst tending flocks on Mt. Ida, and succeeded Hebe in the office of cupbearer to the gods. He is often depicted sitting on the back of a flying eagle.

Gardens, see Pomona.

Gates, see Janus.

Gautama, chief deity of Burmah.

Gellius Aulus, Roman grammarian in the time of M. Antoninus. He wrote "Noctes Atticae" which he composed at Athens.

Genii, domestic deities; every man was supposed to have two accompanying him. One brought happiness, and the other misery.

Genitor, Lycian name of Jupiter.

Geometry, see Mercury.

Germanicus Caesar, son of Drusus and Antonia, niece of Augustus. He was employed in war in Germany where his successes gained him a triumph. He was secretly poisoned, A.D. 19, aged 34. He has been commended for his military talents, learning and humanity.

Geryon, triple-bodied monster living at Gades, where his many flocks were guarded by Orthos, a two-headed dog, and by Eurythion, a seven-headed dragon. These two were destroyed by Hercules, and the cattle driven away.

Gigantes, sons of Coelus and Terra, who, says Hesiod, sprang from the blood of a wound inflicted on Coelus by his son Saturn. They are depicted as huge giants of immense strength.

Girdle, see Cestus.

Glaucus, son of Hippolochus, the son of Bellerophon. He assisted Priam in the Trojan war, and was noted for his folly in exchanging his golden armour with Diomedes for iron armour.

Glaucus, fisherman of Boeotia. He noticed that the fishes he caught and laid on the grass became invigorated and leaped into the sea. He tasted the grass and immediately felt a desire to live in the sea. Oceanus and Tethys made him a sea deity.

Glaukopis, name given to Minerva because she had blue eyes.

Gnomes, name given by Plato to the invisible deities who were supposed to inhabit the earth.

Gnossis, name given to Ariadne, from the city of Gnossus in Crete.

Goat, see Iphigenia, Mendes, and Venus.

Goat's feet, see Capripedes.

Golden Apple, see Atalanta.

Golden Fleece, The, a ram's hide, sometimes described as white, and at other times purple, or golden. It was presented to Phryxus, who took it to Colchis, where King Aeta entertained him, and the hide was hung in the grove of Mars. Jason and forty-nine companions fetched it back. See Argonauts.

Gopya, Indian mythological nymphs.

Gordianus, M. Antonius Africanus, son of Metius Marcellus. He composed a poem in thirty books. He went as proconsul to Africa, and at eighty years of age was proclaimed emperor. He strangled himself at Carthage, A.D. 236, and was lamented by the army and the people.

Gordianus, M. Antonius Africanus, son of the above, was appointed prefect of Rome, and later consul, by Alexander Severus. He was elected joint emperor with his father. He was killed in a battle he fought with Maximinus in Mauritania.

Gordianus, M. Antonius Pius, grandson of the first Gordian, was proclaimed emperor at sixteen years of age. He married the daughter of Misetheus, who was famous for his virtues, and to whom Gordian entrusted the chief offices of state. Gordian conquered Sapor, king of Persia, taking many cities from him. He was assassinated, A.D. 244.

Gordius, a Phrygian peasant who was raised to the throne in consequence of a prediction of the oracle. The knot which tied the yoke to the draught-tree of his chariot was tied so cunningly that the ends of the cord could not be seen, and a report arose that the empire of Asia was promised by the oracle to him who should untie the Gordian knot. Alexander cut the knot with his sword.

Gorgones (the Gorgons), three sisters, daughters of Phorcys and Ceto, whose names were Stheno, Euryale, and Medusa. They had the power to petrify all upon whom they looked. Instead of hair their heads were covered with vipers. Perseus attacked them and cut off Medusa's head, which he gave to Minerva, who set it upon her aegis, which turned into stone all who looked thereon.

Gracchus, T. Sempronius, was twice consul and once censor. His wife Cornelia was a woman of piety and learning of the Scipio family. Their sons Caius and Tiberius were obstinate in their attachment to the interests of the populace, which proved fatal to them. The Gracchi stand out in the annals of Rome. The life of Caius Gracchus was dramatised by J. Sheridan Knowles.

Graces, The, attendants of Venus. Their names were: Aglaia, so called from her beauty and goodness; Thalia, from her perpetual freshness; and Euphrosyne, from her cheerfulness. They are depicted as three cheerful maidens with hands joined, nude or only wearing transparent gowns, signifying that kindnesses, as personified by the Graces, should be done with sincerity and candour, and without disguise.

Graces (Fourth), see Pasithea.

Gradivus, name given to Mars by the Romans. It signified the warrior who defended the city against external enemies.

Gragus, name by which Jupiter was worshipped in Lycia.

Granaries, see Tutelina.

Grapsios, a Lycian name of Jupiter.

Grasshopper, see Tithonus.

Grief, see Niobe.

Gymnasium, place of public exercises in Greece where dancers and wrestlers exhibited and poets and philosophers repeated their compositions.

H

Hada, Babylonian Juno.

Hades, see Ades.

Hailstorms, see Nuriel.

Halcyone, one of the Pleiades, daughter of Atlas and Pelione.

Halcyons, sea-birds, thought to be Greek king-fishers; they made their nests on the waves, and during incubation the sea was always calm. Hence halcyon days.

Halicarnassus, coastal city of Asia Minor, containing a mausoleum which was one of the seven wonders of the world. It was the birthplace of Herodotus, Dionysius, and Heraclitus.

Hamadryades, nymphs who lived in the country and presided over trees.

Hamilcar, celebrated Carthaginian, father of Hannibal. He fought in the first Punic war. He used to tell his three sons that he kept three lions to devour the Roman power.

Hannibal, famous Carthaginian general, son of the above. As a child he swore never to be at peace with Rome. He crossed the Alps with a great army, softening the rocks with fire and vinegar, so that even his elephants descended the mountains without difficulty. He defeated the Romans at Cannae, but was later beaten by Scipio at Zama. He died by poison from his ring in which he had concealed it. He died, B.C. 182, aged seventy.

Happiness, see Genii.

Harmodius, friend of Aristogiton who aided in delivering his country from the tyranny of the Pisistratidae.

Haroeris, Egyptian god, whose eyes were the sun and moon.

Harpies, animals with heads and breasts of women, the bodies of birds, and the claws of lions. They were called Aello, Ocypete, and Celeno. These loathsome creatures lived in filth, poisoning all with which they came in contact. They were daughters of Neptune and Terra.

Harpikruti, Egyptian name for the god Harpocrates.

Harpocrates, son of Isis, and god of silence and meditation. He is depicted as a young man, holding a finger to his lips, and holding a cornucopia in his other hand.

Harvest, see Segesta.

Hasdrubal, son of Hamilcar, and brother of Hannibal. He crossed the Alps and was defeated by the consuls M. Livius Salinator and Claudius Nero. He was slain in battle B.C. 207; his head was sent to Hannibal.

Hawk, see Nysus.

Hazis, Syrian war-god.

Health, see Hygeia and Salus.

Heaven, Queen of, see Belisama.

Hebe, daughter of Jupiter and Juno, was goddess of youth. In her capacity of cup-bearer to the gods she fell down clumsily while pouring out nectar at a festival, and was dismissed from office by Jupiter. Ganymedes succeeded her in office.

Hecate, two goddesses were so named but the one usually mentioned is Hecate, or Proserpina, a name by which Diana was known in the infernal regions. In heaven her name was Luna.

Hector, son of King Priam and Hecuba, was bravest of all Trojan chiefs fighting the Greeks. He wed Andromache, daughter of Eetion, and they had a son, Astyanax. Hector was chief of the Trojan forces when Troy was besieged, and no less than thirty-one of the Greek chiefs were killed by him, but meeting Achilles he fled. Achilles pursued him, and Hector was slain, and his body dragged in triumph at the chariot wheels of the conqueror.

Hecuba, daughter of Dymas, a prince of Phrygia, or some state, of Cisseus, a king of Thracia; she was second wife of Priam, king of Troy. When her son Paris was born, she exposed him on Mt. Ida, meaning him to perish, as it had been predicted that he would cause his country's ruin. Most of her children perished in the Trojan war.

Heifer, see Ino.

Helena, one of the most beautiful women of her time. Even from infancy she was so attractive that Theseus, and his friend Pirithous, abducted her when ten years old and concealed her, but she was recovered by Castor and Pollux, who restored her to her native country. She wed Menelaus, son of Atreus, but Paris persuaded her to fly with him to Troy, B.C. 1198. Menelaus sent messengers to the court of Priam to demand her return, but in vain; this resulted in the Trojan war. After the fall of Troy she returned to Menelaus, and on his death retired to Rhodes, where Polyxo ordered her to be strangled.

Heliades, daughters of Sol, and sisters of Phaeton, at whose death they were so sad that they stood mourning until they changed into poplar trees, and their tears became amber.

Helicon, mountain of Boeotia on the borders of Phocis, sacred to the Muses who had a temple there. The fountain Hippocrene flowed from this mountain.

Heliconides, a name of the Muses, from Mt. Helicon.

Heliogabalus, M. Aurelius Antoninus, Roman emperor who had been a priest of one of the gods of Phoenicia. During his rule Rome became very depraved. He made his horse a consul, and indulged in absurdities which made him odious to his subjects. His soldiers beheaded him, A.D. 222.

Heliopolis, the city of the sun in Elysium.

Helios, Greek sun-god who returned home each evening in a golden boat which had wings.

Heliotrope, Apollo turned Clytie into this flower.

Helle, daughter of Athamas and Nephele, who fled from her father's house to avoid the oppression of her mother-in-law Ino. Some writers state that she rode away in the air on the back of a golden ram and becoming giddy fell into the sea and was drowned. The strait into which she fell received the name of Hellespont from this incident.

Hellespontiacus, a title of Priapus.

Hellespontus, narrow strait between Europe and Asia, so named

from the incident mentioned above. It is celebrated as the scene
of Leander's love and death.

Hemphta, Egyptian equivalent of Jupiter.

Hephaestos, the Greek Vulcan.

Hera, the Greek name of Juno.

Heraclitus, famous Greek philosopher of Ephesus about B.C.
500. He was called the Obscure Philosopher, and the Mourner,
because he used to weep at the follies and frailties of human life.

Herculaneum, town of Campania swallowed by an earthquake,
caused by an eruption of Vesuvius.

Hercules, famous hero, son of Jupiter and Alcmena. Juno hated
him from birth, and before he was eight months old sent two serpents to destroy him; these he seized and crushed to death. When
he grew up his master Eurystheus set him what were thought to
be twelve impossible tasks, which became known as the "Twelve
Labours of Hercules." They were as follows:

1. To slay the Nemean lion.
2. To destroy the Lernaean Hydra.
3. To bring to Eurystheus the Arcadian Stag with golden
   horns and brazen hoofs, remarkable for his swiftness.
4. To seize alive the Boar of Erymanthus, which had committed great ravages.
5. To cleanse the stable of King Augeas, in which 3,000 oxen
   had been housed for thirty years.
6. To kill the carnivorous birds near Lake Stymphalis.
7. To capture the prodigious bull which was desolating Crete.
8. To obtain the mares of Diomedes, which breathed out fire,
   and ate human flesh.
9. To procure the girdle of Hippolyta, queen of the Amazons.
10. To bring to his master the flesh-eating oxen of Geryon, the
    monster king of Gades.
11. To obtain some of the golden apples from the Garden of
    the Hesperides.
12. To fetch from Hades the three-headed dog, Cerberus.

These tasks he successfully accomplished. In addition he aided the
gods in their wars with the Giants, and performed many other

difficult feats, some of which are mentioned under other head-
ings, e.g. Antaeus, Cacus, etc. He was taken by Mercury to Omphale, queen of Lydia, whom he married, and permitted to assume
his armour while he was sitting to spin with her female servants.
He delivered Dejanira from the Centaur, Nessus, whom he killed.
The Centaur, as he was expiring, gave Dejanira a mystic tunic,
which, in a jealous paroxysm, she gave to Hercules to put on. No
sooner had he done this than he was seized with a desperate illness which was incurable. He built a burning pile on Mt. Oeta,
on which he cast himself. Jupiter surrounded the burning funeral
pile with smoke, amidst which Hercules, after his body was consumed, was taken to heaven in a chariot drawn by four horses.

Herdsmen, see Bubona.

Hermae, statues of Hermes, set up in Athens for boundary
marks, and direction marks for travellers.

Hermanubis, see Anubis.

Hermathenae, statues of Mercury and Minerva placed together.

Hermes, Greek name of Mercury.

Herminius, brave Roman who defended the bridge with Cocles
against the army of Porsenna.

Hermione, daughter of Mars and Venus; she married Cadmus.
She was changed into a serpent and allowed to live in the Elysian
Fields.

Another Hermione was daughter of Menelaus. She was be-
trothed to Orestes, but she was abducted by Pyrrhus, son of
Achilles.

Hermippus, a freedman who was a disciple of Philo in the days
of Adrian, by whom he was greatly esteemed. He wrote a number
of books on dreams.

Hermocrates, a general of Syracuse. He was dispatched against
the Athenians. His clemency to prisoners was regarded with suspicion. He was banished, and killed on his attempted return.

Hermodorus, philosopher of Ephesus, said to have assisted as
interpreter in the composition of the ten tables of the laws by the
Roman decemvirs, which tables had been collected in Greece.

Hero, a beautiful girl of Sestos who was a priestess of Venus.

Leander, a youth of Abydos, was much in love with her. They became greatly attached to one another, and often at night Leander swam across the Hellespont to be with Hero in Sestos. One stormy night he was drowned, and in despair Hero threw herself into the sea and perished.

Herodes, surnamed the Great, was made king of Judaea, aided by Antony. After the battle of Actium he continued in power by submission to Augustus. He was notorious for cruelty, and knowing the people would rejoice at his death, he ordered a number of his most important subjects to be confined, and to be murdered immediately on his death, that it might appear that tears were being shed over his own death. He died aged 70, after reigning forty years.

Herodotus, famous historian of Halicarnassus, ranking among historians as Homer does among the poets, and Demosthenes among the orators. His history of the Persian wars against the Greeks from Cyrus to Xerxes is his greatest work. Also a life of Homer has been attributed to him.

Heroes, see Valhalla.

Hesiodus, famous poet of Ascra in Boeotia living in the days of Homer, in competition with whom he gained a poetical prize. Some writers, however, state that Hesiod lived before the age of Homer. His poetry was accounted less sublime than that of Homer, but he was much admired for the elegance of his diction.

Hesione, daughter of Laodemon, king of Troy. She was fated to be exposed to a sea-monster to whom the Trojans presented a young girl each year with a view to appeasing the resentment of Apollo and Neptune, whom Laodemon had offended. Hercules attacked the monster as he was about to devour her, killing him with a club.

Hesperides, three nymphs, daughters of Hesperus. Apollodorus mentions four, Aegle, Erythia, Vesta, and Arethusa. They were guardians of the golden apples Juno gave to Jupiter on their wedding day. The Hesperides lived in a celebrated garden, abounding with delicious fruit, and guarded by a dragon which never slept.

One of the "Labours of Hercules" was to procure some of the golden apples, which he did after slaying the dragon.

Hesperus, brother of Atlas, who was changed into the evening star.

Hestia, Greek name of Vesta.

Hieroglyphics, see Mercury.

Hieronymus, tyrant king of Italy, who became king at fifteen years of age.

Hieronymus, a Christian writer, commonly known as St. Jerome. He showed great zeal against the heretics. He wrote commentaries on St. Matthew's Gospel and on the prophets, etc. He died, A.D. 420, aged eighty.

Highways, see Janus.

Hildur, the Scandinavian Mars.

Hipparchus, son of Pisistratus, who succeeded his father as tyrant at Athens, with his brother Hippias. He was patron of some of the literary men of his day and a lover of literature.

Hippias, a name of Minerva.

Hippius, a name of Neptune.

Hippocampus, Neptune's favourite horse.

Hippocrates, famous physician of Cos, who delivered Athens from a pestilence at the beginning of the Peloponnesian war, and was rewarded with a golden crown. He died, B.C. 361, aged ninety-nine.

Hippocrene, a fountain of Boeotia, near Mt. Helicon, sacred to the Muses. It sprang from the ground when struck by the feet of the horse Pegasus.

Hippocrenides, name given to the Muses, from the fountain of Hippocrene.

Hippodamia, daughter of Oenomaus, king of Pisa, who married Pelops, son of Tantalus. Her father would give her only to one who should conquer him in a chariot race. As she was of great beauty there were many competitors, in spite of the fact that failure involved death. Thirteen were defeated before Pelops entered the lists, but by bribing the charioteer he gained the victory and won Hippodamia.

Hippolyte, Queen of the Amazons, and daughter of Mars. Her father gave her a famous girdle, which Hercules was sent to procure. She was conquered by Hercules, and given by him to Theseus in marriage.

Hippolytus, son of Theseus and Hippolyte. His stepmother Phaedra fell in love with him, and he fled to the sea-shore, where his horses took fright and rushed among the rocks, breaking his chariot to pieces; he was killed. Some say he was restored to life by Diana.

Hippona, a rural deity, goddess of horses.

Hipponax, Greek poet, born at Ephesus, B.C. 540. He was a satirical poet, writing with beauty and vigour.

History, see Cli, and Saga.

Homerus, famous Greek poet. First of all profane writers, he is thought to have lived about 168 years after the Trojan war. No less than seven cities claimed to be his birthplace: Smyrna, Chios, Colophon, Salamis, Rhodos, Argos, and Athenae. The famous Iliad and Odyssey display his consummate knowledge of human nature, and rendered him immortal by the sublimity and elegance of their poetry. The Iliad contains a narrative of the siege of Troy, and the Odyssey deals with the wanderings of Ulysses after the fall of the city.

Honey, see Aristaeus and Dryads.

Honorius, emperor of the Western Empire, son of Theodosius, whom he succeeded. He allowed his generals to conquer his enemies and suffered his ministers to govern his people, which led to his indolence being taken advantage of. He died A.D. 423.

Hope, see Pandora.

Horae, daughters of Sol and Chronis.

Horatii, three Romans born at the same time, who fought the three Curiatii about B.C. 667. Two of the Horatii were killed at the beginning of the fight, and the survivor, pretending to flee, separated his antagonists as they pursued him. Attacking them singly, he slew them all.

Horatius, Q. Flaccus, famous poet born at Venusia. He claimed the attention of Virgil and Varius, who recommended him to the care of Maecenas and Augustus, all celebrated patrons of literature. Under their patronage Horace gave himself to indolence and pleasure. He was a warm friend, who if he gave offence at any time was ready to make any concession to effect a reconciliation. His writings display much wit and satirical humour. He died, B.C. 8, aged fifty-seven.

Horatius, see Cocles.

Horse, see Cyllaros.

Horse Races, see Neptune.

Horses, see Hippona.

Hortensis, a name given to Venus from her care of plants and flowers in gardens.

Hortensius, Q., famous orator who was distinguished in the Roman Forum at the early age of nineteen. Cicero praises his oratorical powers and his retentive memory. Quintilian also praises him highly.

Horus, a name of Sol, the Egyptian god of day.

Hostilina, rural divinity, goddess of growing corn.

Hunger, see Erisichthon.

Hunting, see Diana.

Huntsmen, see Pan.

Hyacinthus, son of Amyclas and Diomede, greatly beloved by Apollo and Zephyrus. He was accidentally killed with a quoit by Apollo, who changed his blood into a flower which bore his name.

Hyades, the seven daughters of Atlas and Aethra, who form the constellation which, when it rises with the sun, threatens rain.

Hybla, a mountain in Sicily, famous for its scented herbs and honey.

Hydra, famous monster serpent, which had many heads. It infested the neighbourhood of Lake Lerna in Peloponnesus. It was one of the "Labours of Hercules" to destroy the monster, which he accomplished with the aid of Iolas.

Hygeia, goddess of health, daughter of Aesculapius and Epione. She was depicted as a young woman feeding a serpent, which is twined round her arm.

Hylas, beautiful boy beloved by Hercules. The nymphs being jealous of him spirited him away while he was drawing water for Hercules.

Hymenaeus or Hymen, Greek god of marriage, son of Bacchus and Venus, or some say, of Apollo and one of the Muses. He is depicted as a handsome lad, holding a burning torch.

Hymettus, a mountain of Attica, near Athens, famous for bees and honey.

Hymn, see Paean.

Hyperion, son of Coelus and Terra, was a model of manly beauty, who married Thea. Aurora was their daughter. Poets often made Hyperion the personification of the sun.

Hypermnestra, one of the Danaides, the fifty daughters of Danaus. Her father ordered her to kill her husband Lynceus on their wedding night. This she refused to do. Danaus eventually forgave her and left his kingdom to Lynceus.

Hypsipyle, queen of Lemnos, and daughter of Thoas. The altars of Venus having been slighted during her reign the goddess punished the Lemnian women by causing their husbands' affections to be estranged. The angry women killed their male relations, except in the case of Hypsipyle, who spared her father Thoas.

I

Iacchus, a name of Bacchus.

Iapetos, father of Atlas. See Japetus.

Iblees, the Satan of Arabia.

Icarus, son of Daedalus, who with his father made wings and flew from Crete to escape the anger of Minos. Icarus flying too high, the sun melted the wax which secured his wings, and he fell into the sea and perished.

Ichnobate, one of Actaeon's hounds, the name signifying a tracker.

Idaea, a name of Cybele, from Mt. Ida, where she was worshipped.

Idaean Mother, name by which Cybele was sometimes called.

Idalia, a name of Venus, from Mt. Idalus.

Idomeneus, son of Deucalion, king of Crete, whom he succeeded. He joined the Greeks in the Trojan war, rendering himself famous for valour. When returning a storm overtook him, and he vowed to Neptune that if he escaped he would offer up to the god the first living creature on which his eyes rested on his arrival at Crete. Arriving in safety, the first person he saw was his son. He kept his vow but had to leave his dominions on account of making himself odious in the eyes of his subjects.

Ignatius, bishop of Antioch thrown to the lions at Rome, A.D. 107. He wrote a letter to the Ephesians, Romans, etc. He was a zealous supporter of the doctrine of the divinity of Christ.

Ilus, fourth king of Troy, and son of Tros and Callirrhoe. He married Eurydice, daughter of Adrastus. He improved the city of Ilium, also called Troy, after his father Tros.

Imperator, a name of Jupiter, given to him at Praeneste.

Inachus, one of the earliest demigods.

Incendiary, see Erostratus.

Incense, see Venus.

Incubus, Roman name of Pan, meaning the Nightmare. See Innus.

Indigetes, deified mortals, gods of the fourth order. They were peculiar to some district.

Indra, Hindoo Jupiter. His wife was Indrant who presides over thunder and winds.

Infants, see Natio.

Innus, a name of Pan, the same as Incubus.

Ino, second wife of Athamas, king of Thebes, father of Phryxus and Helle. Ino had two children, who could not succeed while Phryxus and Helle lived. So Ino persecuted them to such a degree that they determined to flee. This they did on a ram, whose hide became the Golden Fleece. Ino destroyed herself, and Neptune changed her into a sea-goddess.

Inoa, festivals in memory of Ino.

Instrumental Music, see Euterpe.

Io, daughter of Inarchus, and a priestess of Juno at Argos. Jupiter courted her, and was detected by Juno, when the god turned Io into a beautiful heifer. Juno demanded the beast of Jupiter, setting the hundred-eyed Argus to watch her. Jupiter persuaded Mercury to destroy Argus, and Io was released, and restored to human shape. Juno continued to persecute her, and Io roamed from place to place until she arrived at Egypt where she married Telegonus, king of Egypt, or some say Osiris, and treated the people with such kindness that after death she received divine honours, being worshipped as the goddess Isis.

Iolas or Iolaus, son of Iphiclus, king of Thessaly, who assisted Hercules in the slaying of the Hydra. With a hot iron he burnt the place where the heads had been to prevent their regrowth. For accomplishing this he was restored to youth by Hebe. Lovers used to frequent his monument at Phosis to ratify their vows of fidelity.

Iothun, monsters of Celtic mythology.

Iphiclus, son of Amphitryon and Alcmena, and twin brother of Hercules. Juno being jealous of Hercules sent two large serpents to destroy him as the twins lay together in the cradle. Iphiclus was greatly alarmed, but Hercules seized them, one in either hand, and squeezed them to death.

Iphicrates, famous Athenian general, son of a shoemaker, who rose to the highest offices of state. He fought the Thracians, and assisted the king of Persia against Egypt.

Iphigenia, daughter of Agamemnon and Clytemnestra. When the Greeks were on their way to the Trojan war, they were held up at Aulis by contrary winds. A soothsayer told them that in order to appease the gods they must sacrifice Iphigenia to Diana. As the knife was about to enter her body, she suddenly vanished, and a beautiful goat was found in her place.

Iphitus, son of Eurytus, king of Oechalia. When his father promised his daughter Iole to the one who could excel him or his sons in drawing a bow, Hercules made the attempt and was victorious. Eurytus refused to fulfill his compact. Later some oxen were stolen from him and Iphitus was sent to seek them. As he did so he met Hercules, who assisted him, but on remembering the breach of faith of Eurytus, he killed Iphitus.

Irenaeus, a Greek disciple of Polycarp, and bishop of Lyons. He was martyred, A.D. 202.

Iris, one of the Oceanides, messenger of the gods, and more particularly Juno. Her office was to sever the thread which seemed to detain the soul of those who lay dying. She is the personification of the rainbow.

Isis, famous Egyptian deity, daughter of Saturn and Rhea, according to Diodorus. Some suppose her to be the same as Io, who was changed into a heifer, and restored to human form in Egypt, where after her death she received divine honours.

Isocrates, famous orator, son of a musical instrument maker at Athens. He started a school of elocution at Athens which attracted many distinguished pupils. He was a friend of Philip of Macedonia, but the ambition of Philip displeased him, and the defeat of the Athenians at Chaeronea had such an effect upon him that he only survived for a short time. He died about B.C. 338, aged ninety-nine. A brazen statue was erected in his honour by Timotheus, one of his pupils, and Aphareus, his adopted son.

Itys, son of Tereus, king of Thrace, and Procne, daughter of Pandion, king of Athens. When six years of age he was killed by his mother, and served up as food for his father. The gods were enraged and turned him into a pheasant, Procne into a swallow, and Tereus into an owl.

Ixion, king of Thessaly, son of Phlegias. (Hyginus says he was son of Leontes, Diodorus says Antion.) Jupiter carried him to heaven and placed him at the table of the gods, where he fell in love with Juno. This so enraged Jupiter that he banished him from heaven, and ordered Mercury to tie him to a wheel in hell which forever turned over a river of fire.

J

Jani, place in Rome where there were three statues of Janus. It was the meeting place of creditors and usurers.

Janitor, a title of Janus, from the gates before the doors of private houses being known as Januae.

Janus, ancient king of Italy. He was a native of Thessaly, and some writers make him the son of Apollo, others Coelus. He built the town of Janiculum. He is depicted with two faces because he was acquainted with the past and future. He presided over highways, gates, and locks. His temple was always open in time of war, and closed when peace reigned.

Japetus, son of Coelus, or Titan, and Terra; he married Clymene, or some say Asia. The Greeks regarded him as the father of all mankind. See Iapetus.

Jason, famous hero, son of Aeson, king of Ioclos, and Alcimedes. The Centaur Chiron had charge of his education. His greatest recorded feat is his voyage in the Argo to Colchis to fetch the Golden Fleece, which feat he accomplished aided by Juno (see Argonauts). With forty-nine companions he arrived at Colchis, but King Aetes agreed to restore the Golden Fleece only under certain conditions. Jason was to tame the wild fiery bulls and with them plough the field of Mars; to sow the teeth of a serpent from which would spring armed men who would fight against him who sought to plough the field of Mars; to kill the dragon which guarded the tree on which the Golden Fleece was hung. The fate of the Argonauts seemed certain; but Medea, daughter of Aetes, king of Colchis, fell in love with Jason, who vowed eternal fidelity to her. She, being a powerful magician, gave him charms to protect him from danger. After securing the

Fleece, Jason set sail with Medea, whom he had married. The king sent his son Absyrtus to overtake the fugitives, but Medea slew him, strewing his limbs in his father's path, so that he might be delayed in collecting them, thus enabling them to escape. After some years Jason fell in love with Glauce, daughter of Creon, king of Corinth; having divorced Medea he married Glauce. Medea revenged herself for this cruel act by destroying her children in the presence of their father. Jason is said to have been killed by accident by a beam which fell on his head as he was resting by the ship which had taken him to Colchis.

Jocasta or Epicasta, daughter of Menoeceus, wife of Laius, king of Thebes, who married her own son, Oedipus, not knowing who he was. When she discovered this she hanged herself.

Josephus, Flavius, celebrated Jew of Jerusalem who distinguished himself in a siege by Vespasian and Titus of a small town in Judaea. He was in Jerusalem when it was besieged by Titus, and received all the sacred books from the conqueror's hands. He wrote a history of the Jewish wars in Syriac, afterwards translating it into Greek. He also wrote a work, in twenty books, on Jewish antiquities. He died, A.D. 93, aged fifty-six.

Jove, a common name of Jupiter.

Jovianus, Flavius Claudius, native of Pannonia who was elected emperor of Rome by the soldiers after the death of Julian. At first he refused to act, but being assured that his subjects were favourably disposed towards Christianity he accepted. He died after reigning for only seven months, being suffocated, whilst in bed, by charcoal fumes. He died A.D. 364.

Juba, king of Numidia and Mauritania who supported Pompey against Julius Caesar. He defeated Curio, when Caesar had him sent to Africa, and after the battle of Pharsalia he joined forces with Scipio. He was overcome in a battle at Thrapsus, and took his own life. His kingdom became a Roman province, with Sallust as its first governor.

Juba, the second of that name, was taken captive to Rome to give lustre to the triumph of Caesar. His history of Rome is often quoted by the ancients.

Judges in Hell, were Rhadamanthus for Asiatics; Aeacus for Europeans; Minos was the presiding judge. See Triptolemus.

Jugatinus, one of the nuptial deities.

Jugurtha, famous Numidian who went with an army to the aid of Scipio who was besieging Numantia. He endeared himself to the Roman general by his bravery. His uncle Micipsa made him successor to his throne, with his two sons Adherbal and Hiempsal, the latter being killed by Jugurtha, while the former fled to Rome for safety. Caecilius Metellus was sent against Jugurtha, who was delivered to the Romans by betrayal. He died in prison, B.C. 106.

Julia, daughter of Julius Caesar and Cornelia, renowned for virtue and charm. Her father ordered her to divorce her first husband, and marry Pompey the Great, with the object of cementing a friendship between the two men.

Julia, daughter of Germanicus and Agrippina, born at Lesbos, A.D. 17. Her husband was M. Vinicius, a senator. She was exiled on suspicion of conspiracy by her brother Caligula. She was notorious for licentious conduct and was put to death when she was about twenty-four years old.

Julia, famous Phoenician. She studied philosophy, and was noted for mental and personal charm. She came to Rome and married Septimius Severus, who later became emperor. She was also known as Domna.

Julianus, son of Julius Constantius, the brother of Constantine the Great, born in Constantinople. The massacre which followed the succession of Constantine's sons to the throne proved fatal to Julian and his brother Gallus. They had been privately educated in the Christian tradition, which Julian later disavowed, thus he is usually named the "Apostate." He died A.D. 363, aged thirty-two. His last moments were spent with a philosopher discussing the immortality of the soul.

Juno, famous ancient deity, daughter of Saturn and Ops. She wed Jupiter with great solemnity in the presence of all the gods. By her marriage she became queen of the gods and mistress of heaven and earth. She presided over marriage, and was patron of female virtue. Juno was mother of Mars, Vulcan, Hebe, and

Lucina. She incited the gods to conspire against Jupiter, but was frustrated, and Apollo and Neptune were banished from heaven by Jupiter. In competition for the famous Golden Apple, which Juno, Venus, and Minerva each claimed as the fairest of the goddesses, Juno was greatly displeased when Paris gave it to Venus. She is usually depicted riding in a chariot, drawn by peacocks, wearing a diadem, and holding a sceptre.

Jupiter, chief of the gods of the ancients. There were three hundred of that name according to Varro. The one said to be the son of Saturn and Ops is the one to whom the actions of the rest have been attributed. Jupiter was educated on Mt. Ida in Crete, in a cave, and nourished with milk of the goat Amalthaea. While still young he made war against the Titans, whom he conquered. The commencement of his reign in heaven was interrupted by the rebellion of the giants who were sons of the earth, and who desired to avenge the death of the Titans. With the assistance of Hercules, Jupiter overcame them. Jupiter married Metis, Themis, Ceres, Euronyme, Mnemosyne, Latona, and Juno. He was universally worshipped. To the Africans he was Ammon; to the Babylonians, Belus; and to the Egyptians, Osiris.

Justice, see Astrea, Nemesis.

Juvenalis, D. Junius, poet born at Aquinum in Italy. He came to Rome early in life and commenced to write satires, some of which remain. He died A.D. 128. His writings have a lively style but are often ill-humoured.

K

Kali, Hindoo goddess, after whom Calcutta is named.

Kaloc, one of the greatest of Mexican gods.

Kama, Hindoo god of love.

Kebla, point towards which worshippers look during invocations. Thus the worshippers of Sol turn to the east, while Mohammedans turn towards Mecca.

Kederli, god corresponding to the English St. George in Mohammedan mythology. He is invoked by Turks when they go to war.

Kiun, the Egyptian Venus.

Kneph, god of Egypt, having the head of a ram, and the body of a man.

Krishna, Indian god, the avenger of wrongs. Sometimes called the Indian Apollo.

Krodo, the Saxon Saturn.

Kumara, war-god of the Hindoos.

Kuvera, Hindoo god of riches.

L

Labe, the Arabian Circe, having unlimited power of metamorphosis.

Laberius, J. Decimus, Roman knight, skilled in writing pantomimes. Caesar commanded him to appear on the stage in one of his plays. He resented this and threw out aspersions on Caesar during the performance, and warned the audience against tyranny.

Labour, see Atlas, Hercules.

Labyrinth, see Theseus.

Lachesis, one of the three Fates or Parcae. She presided over futurity, and is depicted as spinning the thread of life, or as holding the spindle.

Lacinia, a name of Juno.

Lactura, one of the goddesses of growing corn.

Ladon, dragon which guarded the apples in the garden of the Hesperides. Also one of Actaeon's hounds was called by this name. Also the river to which Syrinx fled when pursued by Pan, where she was changed into a reed, and where Pan made his first pipe.

Laelaps, one of Diana's hunting dogs, which was turned into stone while pursuing a wild boar. Also the name of one of Actaeon's hounds.

Laertes, king of Ithaca who wed Anticlea, daughter of Autolycus. Ulysses, their son, succeeded to the throne, Laertes retiring to the country, and devoting his time to gardening, in which employment he was found by Ulysses on his return from the Trojan war, after an absence of twenty years.

Lagus, a Macedonian of humble origin who married Arsione, daughter of Meleager. They had a child which Lagus exposed at birth, in the woods, but an eagle fed it and sheltered it with her wings. This child became King Ptolemy the First of Egypt.

Lais, an immoral character, daughter of Timandra and Alcibiades. The Cynic, Diogenes, was one of her admirers and won her heart. She went to Thessaly where the women, jealous of her charms, assassinated her.

Laksmi, Hindoo goddess of wealth and pleasure, and one of the wives of Vishnu.

Lamia, an evil deity, the dread of Greek and Roman children, because she was believed to entice and destroy them.

Laocoon, priest of Apollo, who opposed the admission of the wooden horse to the city in the Trojan war. As punishment two enormous serpents were sent to attack him. This they did while he was sacrificing to Neptune, accompanied by his two sons. The serpents coiling round the three crushed them to death.

Laomedon, son of Ilus, and king of Troy. He married Strymo, who was also called Placia, or Leucippe. Podarces, later known as Priam, was their son. Laomedon built the walls of Troy, aided by Apollo and Neptune.

Lapithus, son of Apollo and Stilbe. He married Orsinome who bore him Phorbas and Periphas, to whose many descendants the name of Lapithae was given. Some of these attended the wedding of Pirithous and Hippodamia, daughters of Adrastus, king of Argos. The Centaurs were also present and quarrelled with the Lapithae, leading to blows and slaughter. Many Centaurs were killed, and the remainder were obliged to retire.

Lares and Penates, sons of Mercury and Lara, or some say, Jupiter and Lamida. They were of the lower order of Roman gods, and presided over homes and families. Their statues were usually set within the doors of houses, or near the hearths. Lamps were sacred to them, as symbols of vigilance. The dog was their sacrifice.

Lark, see Scylla and Nysus.

Latinus, son of Faunus and Marica, king of the Aborigines in Italy, who were called Latini after him.

Latona, daughter of Coeus, the Titan, and Phoebe, mother of

Apollo and Diana. Being admired by Jupiter, Juno became jealous, and Latona was the object of her continuous persecution.

Laughter, see Momus and Venus.

Laurel, see Daphne.

Laverna, goddess of thieves.

Law, see Menu.

Lawgiver, see Nomius.

Laws, see Themis.

Leander, a youth of Abydos, who was passionately in love with Hero, a maiden of Sestos. He used to swim the Hellespont to visit her, and on a stormy night he was drowned. See Hero.

Leather Bottle, see Ascolia.

Leda, daughter of Thespius and Eurythemis, who married Tyndarus, king of Sparta. She is famous for her intrigue with Jupiter. She brought forth two eggs, from one of which sprang Pollux and Helena, and from the other Castor and Clytemnestra. She is stated to have been called Nemesis after her death.

Lemnius, a name of Vulcan.

Lemures, the manes of the dead. The ancients believed that after death the soul wandered over the world disturbing the peace of the living.

Lenaeus, a name of Bacchus.

Leonidas, famous king of Lacedaemon who opposed Xerxes, king of Persia, who had invaded Greece with a great army. A fierce battle was fought at Thermopylae, the entire army of Leonidas consisting of three hundred men who refused to abandon him. This tiny army resisted the vast legions of Xerxes, till a traitor conducted a detachment of Persians by a secret path to the rear of Leonidas' army. His soldiers were cut to pieces, only one escaping.

Lepidus, M. Aemilius, famous Roman triumvir with Augustus and Antony. He sprang from illustrious stock, and was very ambitious. He could not maintain his position as triumvir; he therefore resigned and sank into obscurity.

Lerna, lake near Argos where Hercules conquered the Hydra.

Lethe, a river of hell whose waters were imbided by the souls of the dead which had been confined in Tartarus for a certain period. Those who drank forgot all that they had previously known.

Leucippus, famous philosopher of Abdera, about 420 B.C. He was a disciple of Zeno. Diogenes wrote his life. There were others of the same name.

Leucothea, the name of Ino after her transformation into a sea-nymph.

Levana, deity presiding over new-born infants.

Liakura, Mt. Parnassus.

Liberal Arts, see Minerva.

Liber Pater, a name of Bacchus.

Liberty, see Bacchus.

Libissa, queen of fays and fairies.

Libitina, chief of the funeral deities.

Licentiousness, see Belphegor.

Licinius, C., a tribune of the people famous for intrigues and ability. He was a plebeian, being the first of that class to be raised to the office of master of the horse and dictator. There were other Romans of the same name.

Ligea, Greek syren, or sea-nymph.

Lightning, see Agni.

Lilith, a Jewish myth who is the great enemy to new-born children. She is said to have been Adam's first wife, but refusing to submit to him, she was shut out of Paradise and made a spectre.

Lina, goddess of weaving.

Lindor, shepherd lover of Corydon; a love-sick swain.

Lion, see Atalanta, Chimaera.

Liver, see Tityus and Prometheus.

Locks, see Janus.

Lofen, Scandinavian god, guardian of friendships.

Lofua, Scandinavian goddess, reconciler of lovers.

Loke, Scandinavian Satan, the god of strife, the spirit of evil.

Lotis, daughter of Neptune, who fled from Priapus, only escaping from him by being changed into a lotus plant.

Love, see Cupid, Eros, Venus.

Lucanus, M. Annaeus, born at Corduba, in Spain. He went to Rome at an early age when his talents brought him to the notice of Nero. He entered into a poetical contest with the emperor, and obtained an easy victory, which greatly offended Nero. Lucan was now exposed to much annoyance from the emperor and was persuaded to join in a conspiracy against him. For this he was condemned to death by whatever means he chose. He decided to have his veins opened in a warm bath, and died quoting some lines from his "Pharsalia." This of all his works alone remains.

Lucian, the personification of folly, changed into an ass.

Lucianus, famous author of Samosata. He chiefly wrote forceful dialogues. He died A.D. 180. Some say he was torn in pieces by dogs for his impiety.

Lucifer, a name of the planet Venus. It is called Lucifer when it appears in the morning before the sun; when it appears after sunset it is called Hesperus.

Lucilius, C., a Roman knight, regarded as the first satirical writer amongst the Romans. Only a few verses of his works remain. He died at Naples, B.C. 103.

Lucilius Lucinus, famous Roman who fled with Brutus from the battle of Philippi. He was taken prisoner but his captors spared his life.

Lucina, daughter of Jupiter and Juno. She presided over the birth of children.

Lucretia, famous Roman lady, daughter of Lucretius and wife of Tarquinius Collatinus. Some young Roman nobles at Ardea, among them Collatinus and the sons of Tarquin the Proud, were discussing the virtues of their wives. It was agreed to go to Rome to find out how the wives behaved in their husbands' absence. While the wives of the others were indulging in feasting and dissipation, Lucretia was found in her house employing herself with her servants at domestic work. She was brutally treated by Sextus Tarquinius, a relative of Collatinus, and stabbed herself. This was signal for a rebellion, which resulted in the expulsion of the Tarquins from Rome.

Lucretius, Carus T., famous Roman poet and philosopher. In his poem "De Rerum Natura" the tenets of Epicurus are explained. This poem shows great genius and elegance, but its doctrines have an atheistical leaning. The poet is said to have committed suicide, B.C. 54.

Lucullus, Lucius Licinius, famous Roman militarist noted for luxuriant living. He was born about B.C. 115 and was distinguished for eloquence and philosophy. He was advanced to the consulship, and given the task of planning of the Mithridatic war, in which capacity he displayed great military ability.

Lud, mythological king of the ancient Britons.

Luna, a name of Diana as a celestial deity. See Diana and Hecate.

Lupercus, or Pan, Roman god of fertility; his festivals were called Lupercalia, and his festival day was February 15th.

Lycaonian Food, execrable viands, such as were supplied by Lycaon to Jupiter. To test the divine knowledge he served up human flesh, on discovering which Jove punished him by changing him into a wolf.

Lycian Clowns, were changed into frogs by Latona or Ceres.

Lycurgus, famous lawgiver of Sparta, son of King Eunomus and brother of Polydectes. He succeeded his brother on the throne of Sparta. He enacted laws maintaining a just equilibrium between king and people. He banished luxury and encouraged the arts, and adopted many measures to safeguard the welfare of his subjects. He has been likened to Solon, the famous Athenian legislator.

Lymniades, nymphs who resided in marshes.

Lynceus, son of Aphareus; he was a hunter of the Calydonian boar, and an Argonaut. The personification of sharpsightedness, he could see through the earth and distinguish objects at a great distance. Another of the same name married Hypermnestra.

Lysander, famous Spartan general at the close of the Peloponnesian war. He drew Ephesus from the interest of Athens, and won the friendship of Cyrus the Younger. He fought against the Athenian fleet, destroying all save three ships. This battle was fought 405 B.C. The Athenians lost many men, thus losing their influence over neighbouring states. Lysander was slain in battle, B.C. 394.

Lysimachus, son of Agathocles, and one of Alexander's generals. After the king's death Lysimachus made himself ruler of Thrace, building there the town of Lysimachia.

Lysippus, celebrated statuary of Sicyon. He tried painting but was a born sculptor. He lived about B.C. 325 in the days of Alexander the Great.

M

Macrobius, Latin writer who died A.D. 415. He is famous for his "Saturnalia," a miscellaneous collection of antiquarian and critical literature.

Maeander, famous river of Asia Minor which flowed into the Aegean Sea. It is noted amongst the poets for its windings. The word "meandering" is derived from this source.

Maecenas, or Mecaenas, C. Cilnius, famous Roman knight who made himself immortal by his liberal patronage of learned men. Virgil owed the restitution of his lands to the interference of Maecenas. He is reputed to have written a history of animals, and a life of Augustus. Virgil dedicated his Georgics to him, and Horace his Odes.

Maenades, priestesses of Bacchus.

Magicians, see Telchines.

Magna Dea, a name of Ceres.

Magpies, see Pierides.

Mahasoor, Hindoo god of evil.

Maia, mother of the Grecian Mercury.

Mammon, the god of money.

Manes, name used by the ancients to denote the departed soul. The god of funerals and tombs.

Manlius, Marcus, famous Roman, early distinguished for valour. When Rome was captured by the Gauls, he fled with a body of his countrymen to the Capitol, which he defended when it was surprised at night by the enemy, thereby earning the surname Capitolinus. The geese which awakened him to action were afterward regarded as sacred.

Manuring Land, see Picumnus.

Marathon, village of Attica famous for the victory of the
Athenians and Plataeans over the Persian army, B.C. 490, when
they were under the command of Miltiades.

Marcellus, distinguished Roman in the civil wars of Caesar and
Pompey. He firmly supported the latter. Caesar banished him, but
he was later recalled at the request of the Senate.

Marcellus, Marcus Claudius, celebrated Roman general, the first
to gain an advantage over Hannibal. He conquered Syracuse and
carried the spoils to Rome. He was killed in battle during his fifth
consulship.

Mardonius, one of Xerxes' generals, who was defeated at
Plataea. He was slain, B.C. 479.

Marina, a name of Venus, signifying sea-foam, from her having
been formed from the froth of the sea.

Marius, C., Roman who made himself famous under Scipio at
the siege of Numantia. He was commissioned to terminate the
war against Jugurtha, who was defeated. Later he was elected
consul, and was sent against the Teutones. The war was long continued and Marius had been invested with the consulship a fourth
time before it ended in defeat for the Teutones, a vast number of
them being slain. After being honoured with the consulship for
the seventh time Marius died, B.C. 86. There were others of the
same name but of less note.

Marriage, see Cama, Hymen, Juno, Jugatinus.

Mars, god of war, son of Jupiter and Juno, but according to
Ovid, of Juno alone. The loves of Mars and Venus are famous.
Once while in each other's company, Vulcan enclosed them in a
net from which they could not free themselves without assistance.
Thus they were exposed to the ridicule of the gods till Neptune
intervened, and Vulcan released them. Mars espoused the cause of
the Trojans in their war, defending the favourites of Venus with
great determination.

Marshes, see Lymniades.

Marsyas, famous piper of Celaene in Phrygia. He challenged
Apollo to a trial of skill in music. The Muses were appointed

judges and awarded the palm of victory to Apollo, who tied his antagonist to a tree and flayed him.

Martialis, Marcus Valerius, native of Spain who came to Rome at about the age of twenty-one and became noted for his poetical genius. He wrote fourteen books of epigrams. He died aged seventy-five.

Masinissa, king of a part of Africa who assisted the Carthaginians against Rome, but who later joined the Romans. After defeating Syphax he married Sophonisba, wife of Syphax, which offended the Roman general Scipio. Masinissa induced Sophonisba to poison herself. In the battle of Zama, Masinissa contributed largely to the defeat of Hannibal. He died, B.C. 149, aged ninety-seven.

Matura, rural deity, protector of growing corn at the time of ripening.

Mausolus, king of Caria. His wife Artemisia was grieved by his death and erected one of the grandest monuments of antiquity to his memory. The famous building was accounted one of the seven wonders of the world. It was called "Mausoleum" from whence derives the present day use of the word.

Maximinus, Caius Julius Verus, son of a Thracian peasant, who joined the Roman army, rising in rank until he became emperor, A.D. 235. He was a cruel ruler, and at last was killed by his own soldiers. He was great of stature and strength, being able to break the hardest stone between his fingers.

Maximus, a title of Jupiter as greatest of the gods.

Measures and Weights, see Mercury.

Medea, famous magician, daughter of Aetes, king of Colchis, and niece of Circe. She fell in love with Jason when he came to Colchis in quest of the Golden Fleece. They exchanged oaths of fidelity, and when Jason had finished his task Medea accompanied him to Greece. They lived together in Corinth for ten years happily until Jason fell in love with Glauce, daughter of Creon, king of Corinth. To avenge herself, Medea caused the destruction of Glauce, and killed her two children in his presence.

Medicine, see Apollo.

Meditation, see Harpocrates.

Medusa, one of the three Gorgons, daughter of Phorcys and Ceto. She alone of the Gorgons was subject to mortality. She was noted for her charms and the beauty of her hair, which Minerva changed into serpents. According to some writers the Gorgons were born with snakes on their heads, and with yellow wings and brazen hands. Perseus became famous as the conqueror of Medusa. He cut off her head and set it on the Aegis of Minerva. The head had the power of turning to stone all who looked thereon.

Megaera, one of the three Furies.

Megale, Greek name of Juno.

Meleager, signifying great, famous hero of antiquity who excelled in the expedition of the Argonauts, especially by killing the Calydonian boar.

Melpomene, one of the Muses, daughter of Jupiter and Mnemosyne. She presided over tragedy, and is depicted as a young woman wearing a buskin and holding a dagger.

Memnon, king of Ethiopia, son of Tithonus and Aurora. He came to assist Priam in the Trojan war, bringing ten thousand men. He fought with great courage, killing Antilochus, Nestor's son, on which Nestor challenged him to fight. He refused on account of the challenger's great age, but fought Achilles who killed him. A statue erected to his honour had the property of uttering a melodious sound at sunrise each day.

Memory, see Mnemosyne.

Menander, famous comic poet of Athens, educated by Theophrastus. He wrote 108 comedies, but only a few fragments remain.

Mendes, Egyptian god resembling Pan; he was worshipped in the form of a goat.

Menelaus, king of Sparta, brother to Agamemnon. He married Helen, the most beautiful woman of her time. In the absence of Menelaus, Paris arrived at Sparta and persuaded her to elope with him; this was the cause of the Trojan war. In the tenth year of the war Helen obtained Menelaus' forgiveness, and returned to Sparta with him, where shortly after he died.

Menenius Agrippa, famous Roman who appeased the populace in the infancy of the consular government by telling them the well-known fable of the belly and limbs. He died B.C. 495.

Menippus, Cynic philosopher of Phoenicia, who was originally a slave. Obtaining his liberty, he became notorious as a usurer. He produced thirteen books of satires.

Mentor, faithful friend of Ulysses, and instructor of his son Telemachus. Hence the use of the term "mentor" today.

Menu, Hindoo god of law. See Satyavrata.

Merchants, see Mercury.

Mercurius, son of Jupiter and Maia, was messenger of the gods, and conductor of souls to Hades. He is reputed to have invented weights and measures, and presided over orators and merchants. He was known as a cunning thief, for he stole the bow and quiver of Apollo, the girdle of Venus, the trident of Neptune, the tools of Vulcan, and was therefore called the god of thieves. He is also reputed to have invented the lyre, which he exchanged with Apollo for the Caduceus. There was an Egyptian Mercury called Thot, who taught the Egyptians geometry and hieroglyphics.

Merope, one of the Atlantides, who married Sisyphus, son of Aeolus, and was changed into a constellation.

Merops, king of Cos, who married Clymene, one of the Oceanides. He was changed into an eagle, and placed among the constellations.

Meru, abode of the Hindoo god Vishnu, at the top of a mountain 80,000 leagues high. The Olympus of the Indians.

Messalina, Valeria, a woman notorious for her vices, who married the emperor Claudius, who wearying of her conduct ordered her to appear before him and reply to the accusations brought against her. She attempted to destroy herself, but failing, was slain by one of the tribunes who had been sent to summon her.

Metelli, surname of the Roman family of Caecilii. The most noted were: a general who defeated the Achaeans, took Thebes, and invaded Macedonia; Quintus Caecilius, who was successful against Jugurtha, king of Numidia; Q. Caecilius Celer, who fought with distinction against Catilina and died, B.C. 57, greatly mourned by Cicero, who was one of his friends; L. Caecilius, a tribune in the civil wars of Caesar and Pompey, and who favoured the cause of Pompey; Q. Caecilius, a general who conquered Crete and Macedonia; Metellus Cimber, one of the conspirators against Caesar, giving the signal to attack.

Micipsa, king of Numidia, son of Masinissa, who left his kingdom between his sons, Adherbal and Hiempsal, and his nephew Jugurtha; he died B.C. 119.

Midas, king of Phrygia, son of Gordius or Gorgias. Some say that in his early days he found a treasure to which he owed his opulence and greatness. He showed hospitality to Silenus, in return for which Bacchus permitted him to ask any recompense he chose. He asked that whatever he touched should turn into gold. His wish being granted, the very food he attempted to take turned into gold. He prayed Bacchus to revoke the favour, and was ordered to dip in the river Pactolus, the sands of which were turned into gold by the touch of Midas. Later, because he insisted that Pan was superior to Apollo in singing and playing the flute, his ears were changed into those of an ass by the god.

Milo, famous athlete of Crotona in Italy, said to have carried a bullock on his shoulders for some distance, and to have killed it by a blow of his fist, eating it in one day. In his old age he attempted to uproot a tree, which, when half-cleft, reunited, his hands remaining imprisoned. He was devoured by wild beasts, B.C. 500.

Miltiades, son of Simon, was sent by the Athenians to take possession of the Chersonesus. He seized some of the principal inhabitants of the country, and made himself master in Chersonese, marrying the daughter of Olorus, king of the Thracians. He was present at the battle of Marathon, leading the army. He gained the victory but was refused the olive crown he demanded as a reward. Later he was entrusted with seventy ships with which to punish some islands which had revolted to the Persians. At first he was successful but later, being accused of treason, he was condemned to death, but his sentence was commuted owing to his great services. He died of some incurable wounds while in prison.

Mimallones, the "wild women" who accompanied Bacchus, so named because they mimicked his actions.

Mimir, god of wisdom in Scandinavian mythology.

Mind, see Erinnys.

Minerva, goddess of wisdom, war, and the liberal arts. She sprang, full-grown and armed, from the head of Jupiter, and was immediately accepted in the circle of the gods, becoming the most faithful counsellor of her father. She had great power in heaven. She was able to hurl the thunders of Jupiter, prolong the life of men, and bestow the gift of prophecy. She was known by many names—Athena, Pallas, Parthenos, Tritonia (because she was worshipped near Lake Tritonis), and Hippia (because she first taught mankind how to manage horses), Sais (because she was worshipped there). She is depicted with a helmet, with a large plume, in one hand a spear, in the other a shield with Medusa's head on it. Temples were erected for her worship, one of the most renowned being the Parthenon at Athens. Lord Elgin brought a large collection of sculpture from this building to the British Museum. The collection is known as the "Elgin Marbles."

Minos, king of Crete, son of Jupiter and Europa, who gave laws to his subjects, B.C. 1406. These remained in force in the time of Plato.

Minos, principal of the three judges of hell, before whom the souls appeared to hear their doom.

Minos the Second, son of Lycastes, the son of Minos the First, and king of Crete. He married Pasiphae, daughter of Sol and Perseis.

Minotaurus, famous monster, half man, half bull, for which a number of young Athenians were exacted annually to be devoured. The Minotaur was confined in a famous labyrinth, where at last it was slain by Theseus, who found his way out of the labyrinth by a clue of thread given to him by Ariadne, daughter of King Minos.

Mirth, see Momus.

Misery, see Genii.

Mithra, Persian god, ruler of the universe, corresponding with the Roman Sol.

Mithridates the First, king of Pontus, tributary to the crown of Persia. His struggle for independence proved fruitless, and he was defeated in a battle he had provoked.

Mithridates, surnamed "Eupator," and "The Great." He succeeded to the throne of Pontus when eleven years old. The early part of his reign was marred by ambition and cruelty. At an early age he inured himself to hardships by taking part in manly exercises, and sleeping in the open on bare earth. He was almost continuously at war with the Romans, and these engagements are known as the Mithridatic wars. He ordered all Romans in his dominions to be killed. Plutarch says that 150,000 were massacred in one night, but according to another authority the number was 80,000. Great armies were sent against him in revenge. Eventually Mithridates had to succumb to Pompey, and strained by worry and misfortune he attempted to poison himself, but did not succeed, as the many antidotes to poison he had taken to strengthen his constitution in early days resisted the effect. He ordered one of his soldiers to kill him with a fatal blow of the sword, which was done. He died, B.C. 63, aged seventy-two. He was probably the most formidable foe the Romans ever had. Cicero says he was the greatest monarch ever to sit on a throne. He is said to have subdued twenty-four nations, all of whose languages he spoke fluently. Others of the same name were of inferior note.

Mnemosyne, daughter of Coelus and Terra, mother of the nine Muses. Jupiter assumed the form of a shepherd in order to enjoy her company.

Moakibat, the recording angel of the Mohammedans.

Moloch, Phoenician god to whom human sacrifice was offered, principally children. He is thus figurative of the influence which impels us to sacrifice that which we ought to cherish most.

Momus, the god of sarcasm, who blamed Jove for not having made a window in man's breast that his thoughts might be read. He was driven from heaven in disgrace because of his bitter jests. According to Hesiod he was son of Nox. He is also described as god of mirth and laughter. He is depicted holding an image of Folly in one hand, while raising a mask from his face with the other.

Moneta, name given to Juno by writers who thought her to be goddess of money.

Money-god, see Mammon.

Moon, the moon was called Hecate by the ancients, before rising and after setting, Astarte when in crescent form, Diana when in full. See Luna.

Morpheus, minister to the god Somnus, who could imitate perfectly gestures, manners, and words of mankind. He is also known as god of sleep. He is usually depicted as a sleeping child, of great corpulence, with wings.

Mors, Death, the daughter of Nox.

Moschus, bucolic poet in the days of Ptolemy Philadelphus. He wrote eclogues of great charm and elegance, which have been said to equal Theocritus in merit.

Murena, famous Roman who invaded the territories of Mithridates, at first with some success, but later was defeated. He was honoured with a triumph on his return to Rome.

Musae, the Muses were goddesses presiding over poetry, music, dancing, and all the liberal arts. They were nine in number, being the daughters of Jupiter and Mnemosyne named as follows: Clio, Euterpe, Thalia, Melpomene, Terpsichore, Erato, Polyhymnia, Calliope, and Urania. They resided principally in Mt. Parnassus, at Helicon.

Music, see Apollo, Muses.

Mycenae, town of Argolis said to have been built by Perseus. It obtained its name from Mycene, a nymph of Laconia. The town was destroyed by the Argives.

Mythras, Egyptian name of Apollo.

N

Naiades, inferior deities, presiding over rivers, springs, fountains, and wells. They usually resided in the country, resorting to the woods and meadows near the stream over which they presided. They are depicted as beautiful girls, leaning on an urn, from which water flows. Virgil mentions Aegle as being the fairest. The word Naiad is now in frequent use, especially by poets.

Nandi, Hindoo goddess of joy.

Narae, the Hindoo infernal regions.

Narayan, Hindoo god of tides. The name signifies "the mover of the water."

Narcissus, son of Cephisus and the Naiad Liriope, was a beautiful lad, born at Thespis in Boeotia. He fell in love with his own reflection in the water, supposing it to be the nymph of the place. His futile efforts to reach this object of his desire so angered him that he killed himself. The flower now so named sprang from his blood.

Nastrond, Scandinavian place of eternal punishment.

Natio, Roman goddess, protectress of infants.

Nemaea, town of Argolis, where Hercules slew the famous Nemaean lion when he was only sixteen years of age. It was first of the Labours of Hercules. When he found his arrows and clubs were useless against it, he seized it in his arms and strangled it.

Nemesis, an infernal deity, daughter of Nox, and goddess of vengeance. Some mythologists say she was a Parca. She constantly travelled in search of wickedness, which she punished with great severity. She is sometimes mentioned under the name of Adrastaea. The Romans sacrificed to her before going to war, in signification that they took up arms in the cause of justice.

Neoptolemus, king of Epirus, son of Achilles and Deidamia, also called Pyrrhus. He distinguished himself in the siege of Troy, and he was the first to enter the wooden horse. He was inferior to none of the Greek warriors in valour, and only Ulysses and Nestor were superior to him in eloquence and wisdom.

Nephalia, Greek festivals in honour of Mnemosyne, mother of the Muses.

Nepos, Cornelius, famous historian in the reign of Augustus, who enjoyed, in common with his literary contemporaries, the patronage of the emperor. He was an intimate friend of Atticus and Cicero. He was lively of disposition and displayed a delicacy of sentiment. His "Lives of Illustrious Greek and Roman Generals" is his only existing work.

Neptunus, god of the sea, son of Saturn and Ops, and brother to Jupiter and Pluto. He was devoured by his father as soon as he was born, but restored by a potion given to Saturn, by Metis, first wife of Jupiter. Neptune shared the empire of Saturn with his brothers and received as his portion the kingdom of the sea. Not thinking this equivalent to the empire of heaven and earth, which Jupiter had claimed, he conspired to dethrone him. On discovering the conspiracy, Jupiter condemned Neptune to build the walls of Troy. He wed Amphitrite, who had vowed perpetual celibacy. They had a son called Triton. He was also father of Polyphemus, Phoreus, and Proteus. Neptune is depicted seated in a chariot, drawn by dolphins, and surrounded by tritons and sea-nymphs. He holds a trident with which he rules the waves.

Nereides, aquatic nymphs, daughters of Nereus and Doris. They were fifty in number. They are depicted as beautiful girls, riding on dolphins, and bearing tridents.

Nereus, sea deity, husband of Doris. He foretold fates. He had the power of assuming various shapes which enabled him to escape from the importunities of those anxious to consult him.

Nero, Claudius Domitius Caesar, famous Roman emperor, son of Caius Domitius Ahenobarbus and Agrippina, the daughter of Germanicus. He was notorious for cruelty and vice. At night he was in the habit of leaving his palace to visit the lowest taverns and scenes of depravity. Sometimes he appeared on the stage, representing the meanest characters. He resolved to imitate the burning of Troy, causing Rome to be fired in several places, and the city burned for nine days, while he exulted in the scene. He sang from the top of a tower accompanying himself on a lyre. Conspiracies were formed against him. He was saved from the most dangerous of these by the confession of a slave. He killed himself, A.D. 68, he then being aged thirty-two. He reigned thirteen years and eight months. There were some few who mourned him, and Suetonius records that some unseen hand placed flowers on his tomb.

Nerva, M. Cocceius, Roman emperor succeeding Domitian, A.D. 96. He was popular for his mildness and generosity; he set a good example of manners and sobriety. He made an oath that no senator should be put to death in his reign, and carried it out by pardoning two members of the senate who had conspired against his life. He died, A.D. 98, aged 72. He was succeeded by Trajan, his son.

Nessus, the Centaur which was destroyed by Hercules for insulting Dejanira.

Nestor, son of Neleus and Chloris, grandson to Neptune, and nephew to Pelias. He witnessed the bloody battle between the Lapithae and the Centaurs, which took place at the nuptials of Pirithous. As king of Pylos he led his soldiers in the Trojan war and was a distinguished chieftain. Homer depicts him as the most perfect of all the heroes. After the war Nestor retired to Greece, living his declining years in peace and tranquility. The date and manner of his death are not known.

Nicephorus, name of Jupiter, signifying the bearer of victory.

Nidhogg, dragon dwelling in Nastrund in Scandinavian mythology.

Niflheim, Hell of Scandinavian mythology. It consisted of nine vast regions of ice beneath the North Pole, where darkness reigned eternally.

Night, see Nox.

Nightingale, see Philomela.

Nightmare, see Incubus.

Ninus, son of Belus; he built Nineveh and founded the Assyrian monarchy, B.C. 2059. He married Semiramis, whose first husband had destroyed himself through fear of him. He reigned fifty-two years.

Niobe, daughter of Tantalus, king of Lydia, and Euryanassa or Dione. She is the personification of grief. She married Amphion, and according to Hesiod, had ten sons and ten daughters. By order of Latona the father and sons were killed by the darts of Apollo, and all the daughters, except Chloris, were destroyed by Diana. Niobe, overwhelmed with grief, was turned into a marble statue.

Nitocris, famous queen of Babylon, who built a bridge over the Euphrates in the centre of the city, and dug reservoirs for the superfluous water of the river.

Nomius, one of the names of Apollo, signifying a lawgiver. Applied also to Mercury.

Norns, three Scandinavian goddesses, who wove the woof of human destiny.

Notus, Auster, the south wind.

Nox, one of the most ancient deities among the heathen, daughter of Chaos, and sister to Erebus and Mors. She gave birth to the Day, and the Light, and was mother of the Parcae, Hesperides, Dreams, Death, etc.

Numa Pompilius, famous philosopher of Cures. He married Tatia, daughter of Tatius, king of the Sabines, and at her death retired to the country to devote himself to literary pursuits. When Romulus died the Romans chose him for their king. After at first refusing he was prevailed upon to accept. He tried to inculcate a reverence for the deity, and did all he could to heal the dissensions of his subjects. He dedicated a temple to Janus, which remained closed during his entire reign, as a mark of peace and tranquility at Rome. He died, B.C. 672, after a reign of forty-three years.

Nundina, goddess who took charge of children when nine days old, this being the day on which the Romans named their children.

Nuptialis, a title of Juno. When invoked under this name, the gall of the victim was removed and thrown behind the altar, signifying there should be no bitterness or anger between married people.

Nuriel, god of hailstones in Hebrew mythology.

Nyctelius, name of Bacchus, because his festivals were celebrated by torchlight.

Nymphae, class of inferior female deities who attended the gods. Some presided over springs, fountains, wells, woods, and the sea. There were land-nymphs or Naiads, and sea-nymphs or Nereides, but the former are also associated with fountains and rivers. There were forest-nymphs called Dryades, and the Hama-dryades who lived amongst the oak-trees. The Oreades were mountain nymphs.

Nysae, nymphs by whom Bacchus was nursed. See Dionysius.

Nysaeus, name of Bacchus, because he was worshipped at Nysa.

Nysus, king of Megara who was invisible by virtue of a particular lock of hair. His daughter Scylla, having cut it off, betrayed her father to his enemies. She was turned into a lark, and the king into a hawk, and he still pursues his daughter, intending to punish her.

O

Oannes, Eastern god, half man and half fish. He taught men letters in the daytime, and at night he returned to the depth of the ocean.

Oath, see Lapis.

Obambou, a devil of African mythology.

Ocean, see Neptune.

Oceanides, sea-nymphs, daughters of Oceanus and Tethys. Some writers say that they were as many as three hundred in number, others state as few as sixteen. The principal ones mentioned are Amphitrite, Doris, Metis.

Oceanus, son of Coelus and Terra, and husband of Tethys. Several mythological rivers were said to be his sons. Some ancients worshipped him as god of the seas, invoking his aid when going on a voyage. He was considered to personify the immense stream, which it was supposed surrounded the earth, into which the sun and moon sank daily.

Ocridion, king of Rhodes, deified after death.

Octavia, sister to the emperor Augustus, famous for beauty and virtue. She wed Claudius Marcellus, and, after his death, Antony, who deserted her for Cleopatra.

Octavianus, or Octavius Caesar, famous Roman, who after the battle of Actium, was given the surname Augustus by the senate.

Ocypete, one of the Harpies, who infected everything she touched.

Ocyroe, daughter of Chiron, she had the gift of prophecy, and was changed into a mare.

Odenatus, famous prince of Palmyra. He strengthened his endurance by hunting wild beasts while still very young. He was a faithful ally to Rome, giving great offence to Sapor, king of Persia, in consequence. In the war which ensued he gained victories and took Sapor's wife prisoner; he also gained great spoils. One of his relations, whom he had offended, killed him. Zenobia followed him on the throne.

Odin, god of the universe in Scandinavian mythology, and reputed father of the Scandinavian kings. His wife was Friga, who bore him Thor and Balder.

Oeagrus, father of Orpheus.

Oedipus, son of Laius, king of Thebes, and Jocasta. Laius was told by the oracle that he would perish by the hands of his son. On his birth Oedipus was given to a servant who was told to expose him to death on the mountains, where he was discovered by one of Polybus' shepherds. Periboea, wife of Polybus, educated him with great care. In later life he met Laius in a chariot in a narrow lane. He was haughtily ordered to make way for Laius, and a fight ensued in which Laius was killed. Oedipus now went to Thebes, attracted by the fame of the Sphinx, who devoured all who attempted unsuccessfully to explain the enigmas she propounded. The Sphinx asked Oedipus, "What animal in the morning walks upon four feet, at noon on two, and in the evening on three?" Oedipus solved the riddle by replying that it was man, who in childhood crawls on hands and feet, as a man walks on two feet erect, and in the evening of life supports himself with a staff. The Sphinx, on hearing the correct solution, dashed her head against a rock and died.

Oeneus, king of Calydon, son of Parthaon or Portheus and Euryte. By his wife, Althaea, he had four children, Clymenus, Meleager, Gorge, and Dejanira. He slighted Diana, who sent a wild boar to lay waste his country. Meleager killed the animal in the famous Calydonian boar hunt. Misfortune overtook Oeneus, and he exiled himself, dying on his way to Argolis.

Oenomaus, king of Pisa, in Elis, and father of Hippodamia. The oracle foretold that he would perish by the hands of his son-in-law. He announced that he would give his daughter to whoever could defeat him in a chariot race, death being the penalty to those defeated. After a number had tried without success, Pelops, son of Tantalus, entered the lists and by bribing the charioteer, who provided a chariot with a broken axle-tree, Pelops won the race, married Hippodamia, and became king of Pisa. Oenomaus was killed in the race.

Oenone, wife of Paris, a nymph of Mt. Ida. She had the gift of prophecy.

Ogygia, the island abode of Calypso, so beautiful in sylvan scenery that even Mercury, who resided in Olympus, was charmed with it.

Ointment, see Phaon.

Olenus, daughter of Vulcan, wife of Lethaea, a woman who considered herself more beautiful than the goddesses. As a punishment she and her husband were turned to stone.

Olives, see Aristaeus.

Olympia, famous games, receiving their name either from Olympia, where they took place, or from Jupiter Olympius, to whom they were dedicated.

Olympius, name of Jupiter, from Olympia, where he had a splendid temple, considered to be one of the seven wonders of the world.

Olympus, magnificent mountain in Macedonia and Thessaly. The ancients supposed that it reached the heavens, and so made it the residence of the gods, and scene of Jupiter's court. Eternal spring reigned on the top, according to the poets.

Olyras, river near Thermopylae, which is said to have attempted to extinguish the funeral pile of Hercules.

Omophagia, festival of Bacchus at which uncooked meats were served.

Omphale, queen of Lydia, daughter of Jardanus. Her husband Tmolus bequeathed his kingdom to her. Having heard of the deeds of Hercules she wished to see him. After he had killed Eurytus, Hercules was ordered to be sold as a slave, and was purchased by Omphale, who set him at liberty. He fell in love with her, and became so infatuated that he led an effeminate life in her society, wearing female apparel, while Omphale wore his lion's skin, and armed herself with his club.

Onarus, priest of Bacchus, said to have married Ariadne after she had been abandoned by Theseus.

Onuva, Venus of the ancient Gauls.

Opalia, Roman festivals in honour of Ops, held on the 14th of the calends of January.

Oppianus, Greek poet of Cilicia, who wrote poetry famous for sublimity and elegance. Caracalla gave him a piece of gold for every verse in one of his poems. He died of plague when thirty years old.

Ops, mother of the gods, daughter of Coelus and Terra, the same as Rhea of the Greeks. She married Saturn, and became mother of Jupiter. She had many names, among them the following: Cybele, Bona Dea, Magna Mater, Thya, Tellus, and Proserpine.

Oracles, see Themis.

Oraea, sacrifices offered to the goddesses of the seasons to invoke fair weather for ripening the harvest.

Orbona, goddess of orphans.

Orchards, see Feronia.

Oreads, mountain nymphs, attendant on Diana.

Orestes, son of Agamemnon and Clytemnestra. He was saved from his mother's dagger by his sister Electra, whom Homer calls Laodicea, and was taken to the house of Strophius, king of Phocis, who had married a sister of Agamemnon. Strophius treated him kindly and educated him with his own son Pylades. The young princes formed a firm friendship. When Orestes became a man, he avenged his father's death (who had been slain by Clytemnestra) by killing his mother.

Orgies, riotous feasts of Bacchus were so called.

Origen, Greek writer famous for learning and genius. He was martyred at the age of sixty-nine. He wrote numerous works, many being commentaries on the Scriptures, and various treatises.

Orion, famous giant, blinded by Oenopion for a grievous wrong done to Merope; he was exiled from Chios. The sound of the

Cyclopes' hammers led him to the abode of Vulcan, who gave
him a guide. He consulted an oracle, and had his eyes restored by
fixing his eyes upon the sun. He was later slain by Diana and
placed among the stars, where his constellation is one of the
brightest.

Orithyia, daughter of Erechtheus. Boreas carried her off while
she was wandering by the river Ilissus. The two-winged warriors,
Zetes and Calais, who accompanied the Argonauts, were her sons.

Ormuzd, creator of all things in Persian mythology.

Oros, the Egyptian Apollo.

Orphans, see Orbona.

Orpheus, son of Oeger and the Muse Calliope (some say he was
son of Apollo). Apollo (some say Mercury) gave him a lyre
which he learned to play so masterfully that the strains of his
music caused rivers to cease to flow, and savage beasts to become
docile. He married Eurydice, who perished from the bite of a
serpent. Orpheus was so disconsolate that he visited the infernal
regions with a view to recovering her. Pluto was enraptured with
his music, the wheel of Ixion ceased to turn, Tantalus forgot his
thirst, and even the Furies relented. Pluto consented to restore
Eurydice to him, on condition that he did not look behind him
while he was in his domain. Orpheus agreed but forgot his promise and turned to look at Eurydice, who instantly vanished. After
this he shunned society. The Thracian women, stung by his coldness, attacked him while they celebrated the orgies of Bacchus.
Having torn his body to pieces they threw his head into the
Hebrus.

Osiris, Egyptian god of the sun, worshipped under the form of
an ox. Ancient writers differ when writing of this celebrated god,
but agree that as a ruler of Egypt he took great pains to civilize
his subjects and improve their morals.

Ossa, one of the mountains which the giants piled on top of
Olympus to enable them to reach heaven and attack the gods.

Ovidius, P. Naso, famous Roman poet born at Sulmo. At an
early age he was sent to Rome, later going to Athens where he
studied elocution. His natural bent was poetry, however, and this

became his chief object. His style soon attracted attention and gained learned admirers for him. Virgil, Horace, Propertius, and Tibullus corresponded with him and Augustus became his generous patron. These favours were but transitory, and he was banished to a place on the Euxine Sea by the emperor. The cause of his banishment is unrecorded. His friends entreated for his return in vain, and he died in a few years in A.D. 17, aged 59. Many of his works remain, notably "Metamorphoses," "Fasti," and "Epistolae."

Ox, see Apis.

Owl, see Aesculapius and Itys.

P

Pactolus, river in Lydia in which Midas washed at the order of Bacchus. The sands there were turned to gold at his touch.

Paean, name given to Apollo, derived from PAEAN, a hymn sung in his honour for killing the serpent Python.

Palamedes, a Greek chieftain, son of Nauplius, king of Euboea, and Clymene. The Greek princes, going to the Trojan war, sent him to fetch Ulysses to the camp. Ulysses pretended to be insane in order to miss the expedition. Palamedes discovered the deception, thus obliging Ulysses to join the war. Enmity sprang up between the two and by artifice Ulysses engineered the death of Palamedes. Palamedes is reputed to have invented dice, backgammon, and other games.

Palatinus, Mons, largest of the seven hills on which Rome was built.

Pales, goddess of shepherds and protectress of their flocks. Palilia was the name of her festivals.

Palinurus, pilot of Aeneas' ship, who fell into the sea while he was sleeping, being exposed to the waves three days. On reaching shore he was killed by the natives.

Palladium, famous statue of the goddess Pallas. She holds a spear in her right hand, and a distaff and spindle in the left. Its origin is the subject of various accounts. Some say it fell from heaven near the tent of Ilus as he was building the citadel of Ilium. According to others it fell in Phrygia, while still others state that Dardanus received it as a present from his mother Electra. It is generally agreed that the fate of Troy depended on its preservation. The Greeks, knowing this, obtained possession of it in the Trojan war. Some writers say however that the true Palladium was never taken, but only a statue which had been set near it, and resembled it.

Pallas, a name of Minerva given to her because she slew a famous giant of that name.

Palmyra, capital of Palmyrene, a country on the eastern boundaries of Syria, famous as the seat of government of the famous Queen Zenobia.

Pan, the Arcadian god of shepherds, huntsmen, and rural folk; chief of the lesser deities. The supposed son of Mercury and Penelope, he was metamorphosed, after birth, into the mythical form in which he is represented as a horned, long-eared man, with the lower half of the body resembling a goat. He plays a pipe with reeds of varying lengths, invented by himself, on which he could produce music which charmed the very gods. His appearance once so frightened the Gauls when they invaded Greece that they fled though none pursued them, hence the word panic. He was attended by the Fauns, who resembled him.

Pandarus, son of Lycaon, who assisted the Trojans in their war with Greece. He broke a truce which had been agreed upon between the armies, wounding Menelaus and Diomedes. The latter was later responsible for the death of Pandarus.

Pandion, king of Athens, father of Procne and Philomela. His reign marked a period of such plenty that it was supposed Bacchus and Minerva had visited the country in person.

Pandora, the first mortal female, according to Hesiod. Vulcan formed her of clay, and having received life the gods made presents to her. Venus gave her beauty, and the art of pleasing; the power of captivating was bestowed by the Graces. Apollo taught her to sing, and Mercury instructed her in oratory. Jupiter presented her with "Pandora's Box," which she was ordered to present to her future husband. She wed Epimetheus, brother of Prometheus, and as soon as he opened the box a multitude of evils proceeded to issue therefrom, and became dispersed throughout the world, and since have never ceased to affect mankind. Hope alone remained at the bottom of the box.

Pansa, C. Vibius, Roman consul, who, in company of Hirtius, pursued the assassins of Caesar. He was killed in a battle near Mutina.

Pantheon, Roman temple of all the gods, built in the reign of Augustus, by Agrippa. Its style of architecture was Corinthian, the measurements being: diameter 144 feet, and height 144 feet. It was mostly of marble, its walls being covered with engraved silver and brass. Pliny ranked it among the wonders of the world.

Paphia, a name of Venus.

Papremis, the Egyptian Mars.

Parcae, goddesses, called the Fates, who presided over the birth and life of mankind. Their names were: Clotho, Lachesis, and Atropos, daughters of Nox and Erebus or, possibly, Jupiter and Themis.

Paris, son of Priam, king of Troy, and Hecuba. He was also called Alexander. It was predicted before his birth that he would bring ruin to his country, and his mother dreamed that he would be a torch which would fire her palace. The soothsayer also predicted that he would be the cause of the destruction of Troy. In view of this Priam ordered a slave to destroy the child as soon as it was born, but the slave neglected to do this, and instead exposed the child on Mt. Ida, where shepherds found and tended him. He gave early proofs of courage, and his good looks attracted Oenone, a nymph of Ida, whom he married. At the famous nuptials of Peleus and Thetis, Discordia, goddess of discord, was not invited. To show her displeasure, she attended secretly. When all were present, she threw amongst them a golden apple, on which were written the words, "Let the fairest take it." This caused much contention but at last the claimants were reduced to three, Juno, Venus, and Minerva. It was decided that Paris should act as umpire. The goddesses courted his favour and offered him bribes. Juno offered him power, Minerva wisdom, and Venus promised him the most beautiful woman in the world. Paris gave the apple to Venus. Later Priam owned Paris as his son and sent him to Greece to fetch Helen, reputed to be the most beautiful woman in the world. She was wife of Menelaus, king of Sparta, but during the king's absence Paris persuaded Helen to elope with him.

This led to the Trojan war which ended in the destruction of Troy. Accounts of the death of Paris vary. Some say that he was among the 676,000 Trojans who fell during the siege, others that he was killed by one of the arrows of Philoctetes, which had once belonged to Hercules.

Parmenio, one of Alexander's generals by whom he was regarded with great affection. Their friendship was broken in a sudden fit of temper, when Alexander ordered Parmenio to be put to death, B.C. 330.

Parnassides, name for the Muses, from Mt. Parnassus.

Parnassus, mountain of Phocis sacred to the Muses, and to Apollo and Bacchus. Any who slept on this mountain became poets.

Parrhasius, famous artist of Ephesus in the days of Zeuxis, about B.C. 15. He contended with Zeuxis for the palm of painting, and Zeuxis acknowledged his rival's superiority.

Parthenon, temple of Minerva at Athens. It was destroyed by the Persians and rebuilt by Pericles.

Parthenos, a name of Juno, also of Minerva.

Pasiphae, daughter of Sol and Perseis, and wife of Minos, king of Crete. She was the reputed mother of the Minotaur which was killed by Theseus.

Pasithea, when *four* Graces are mentioned, Pasithea is the fourth.

Patroclus, Greek chieftain during the Trojan war who contracted a friendship with Achilles, living in the same tent with him. When his friend refused to appear on the field of battle, because he was offended with Agamemnon, Patroclus imitated his example. Nestor persuaded him again to take the field, and Achilles lent him his armour. Hector came into contact with him and, after a desperate fight, slew him. The Greeks recovered his body, which was received by Achilles with great lamentation. He again took the field and slew Hector, thus avenging his friend.

Paulus Aemilius, Roman famous for his military achievements. He was called Macedonicus from his conquest of Macedonia. He subjected himself to discipline from an early age. During his first consulship he reduced the Ligurians to subjection, and later obtained a great victory over the Macedonians, and made himself master of the country. As censor he acted with great moderation. He was deeply mourned by the Romans when he died, B.C. 168.

Pausanias, noted Spartan general who distinguished himself at the battle of Plataea, against the Persians. Later, at the head of the Spartan armies, he extended his conquests in Asia, but his haughtiness gained him many enemies. He made an offer, under certain conditions, to betray Greece to the Persians, but his intention being discovered, he fled for safety to the temple of Minerva, where he starved to death, B.C. 471.

Pavan, Hindoo god of the winds.

Peace, see Concordia.

Peacock, see Argus.

Pegasus, winged horse supposed to have sprung from the blood of Medusa. Ovid says he fixed his abode on Mt. Helicon, where by striking the ground with his foot, he raised the fountain called Hippocrene.

Peleus, king of Thessaly, son of Aeacus and Endeis, the daughter of Chiron. He married Thetis, one of the Nereids.

Pelias, son of Neptune and Tyro. After his birth he was exposed in the woods. Some shepherds discovered and tended him. Later Tyro married Cretheus, king of Iolchos, and they had three children, Aeson being the eldest. Pelias visited his mother after the death of Cretheus, and usurped the authority properly belonging to the children of the dead king. Jason, son of Aeson, who had been tutored by Chiron, on attaining manhood, demanded the kingdom. Pelias persuaded Jason to waive his claim for the present, and set forth on the Argonautic expedition. On his return, accompanied by the sorceress Medea, she undertook to restore Pelias to youth, saying it was necessary first to cut his body in pieces and place the limbs in a cauldron of boiling water. This being done, Medea refused to fulfill her promise, which she had solemnly made to the four daughters of Pelias who were called the Peliades.

Pelion, or Pelios, famous mountain of Thessaly, whose top was covered with pine-trees. It was famous for the wars between the giants and the gods, and as the abode of the Centaurs, who were expelled by the Lapithae.

Pelopidas, famous Theban general, son of Hippoclus. The famous victory of Leuctra was won in consequence of his valour and prudence, combined with the ability of Epaminondas.

Pelops, famous prince, son of Tantalus, king of Phrygia, who was killed by his father, and served up as a feast to the gods, who had visited Phrygia. When the gods discovered what had been done they restored him to life. He became the husband of Hippodamia, having won her by defeating her father in a chariot race.

Penates, inferior Roman deities, presiding over domestic affairs. See Lares.

Penelope, famous Grecian princess, daughter of Icarius, and wife of Ulysses, king of Ithaca. She became mother of Telemachus, and with great reluctance, was obliged to part from her husband when the Greeks insisted in his participation in the Trojan war. When after ten years, at the conclusion of the war, Ulysses did not return, her anxiety became overwhelming. She had many suitors who told her that her husband would never return. She received their attentions with coldness, but being almost a prisoner in their hands, she temporised with them. After an absence of twenty years Ulysses returned, and delivered her from the importunities of her suitors. Homer describes Penelope as being a model of female propriety, but accounts by different authors respecting her differ materially. Some claim that she was the mother of Pan.

Penthesilea, queen of the Amazons, daughter of Mars. She assisted Priam in the last years of the Trojan war, and was killed by Achilles.

Pergamus, citadel of the city of Troy. The word is often used to signify Troy.

Pericles, Athenian noble, son of Xanthippus and Agariste. He had great natural ability which was fostered by the lectures of Zeno, and other philosophers. He became commander, statesman, and orator, and was generally esteemed. The prosperity of Athens was his chief concern, and he did not seek to enrich himself in his ministerial capacity. He fought against the Lacedaemonians, and restored the temple of Delphi to the care of the Phocians, who had been improperly deprived of their trust. His ambitious views fomented the Peloponnesian war. Later his popularity waned temporarily, but he was restored to all the honours of which he had been deprived. He died in a pestilence, B.C. 429, aged seventy.

Perpetual punishment, see Sisyphus.

Persephone, Greek name of Proserpine.

Perseus, son of Jupiter and Danae, daughter of Acrisius. The oracle predicted that Acrisius would perish at the hand of his daughter's offspring, so Perseus, and his mother Danae, were thrown into the sea after his birth. Both were preserved and reached the island of Seriphos, and were kindly treated by Polydectes, the king. But the king soon became jealous of the genius of Perseus, who had promised to bring to him the head of the Gorgon Medusa. Pluto lent him a helmet which made the wearer invisible, Minerva gave him her buckler, and Mercury provided him with wings. Thus equipped he found the Gorgons, and cut off Medusa's head, with which he flew through the air. From the blood which dropped from it sprang Pegasus, the winged horse. During his journey Perseus discovered Andromeda chained to a rock to be devoured by a sea monster, which he killed, and married Andromeda. Returning to Seriphos he turned Polydectes into stone by showing him Medusa's head. By accident Perseus killed Acrisius with a quoit, thus fulfilling the oracle's prediction.

Perseus, or Perses, son of Philip, king of Macedonia. He displayed great enmity of the Romans, and made preparations to attack them. He declared war, but lacked sufficient resolution to follow up initial advantages gained by him. He was defeated at Pydna, taken prisoner, and later died in captivity at Rome.

Persius, Aulus Flaccus, poet of Volaterrae. He came from good stock and soon became intimate with the most illustrious Romans of his day. He spent his early life in his native town, removing to Rome at the age of sixteen, where he studied philosophy. He died, A.D. 62, aged thirty.

Persuasion, goddess of, see Pitho.

Pertinax, Publius Helvius, Roman emperor who succeeded Commodus. He came from an obscure family, spending some time as a charcoal burner. He joined the army, and by his valour rose to the highest offices of trust, becoming consul. He was selected to succeed Commodus. His patriotism gained for him the affection of his worthiest subjects, but some plotted against him. He was killed by his soldiers, A.D. 193.

Petronius Arbiter, one of Nero's favourites, and a minister and associate of his pleasures and vices. He was made proconsul of Bithynia, and later honoured with the consulship. He later lost favour with Nero, and destroyed himself by having his veins opened, A.D. 66. He distinguished himself by his writings, being author of many elegant compositions, but these were often characterised by improper language.

Phaedra, daughter of Minos and Pasiphae, who became wife of Theseus, and mother of Acamas and Demophon. She unjustly accused Hippolytus, a son of Theseus before she married him, who was killed by his chariot horses taking fright, causing him to be thrown under the wheels and crushed to death. On hearing this, she acknowledged her false charge and hanged herself in despair.

Phaethon, son of Sol or Phoebus and Clymene. Hesiod and Pausanias state that he was son of Cephalus and Aurora; or of Tithonus and Aurora according to Apollodorus. He is generally accepted as son of Phoebus and Clymene. Phoebus allowed him to drive the chariot of the sun for one day. Phaethon displayed complete incapacity; the horses becoming unmanageable, heaven and earth were threatened with a conflagration. Jupiter struck Phaethon with a thunderbolt, and hurled him into the River Po, where he perished.

Phalaris, a tyrant of Agrigentum. Perillus made him a brazen bull inside which he proposed to place culprits, and by applying fire, burn them to death. The first victim was Perillus himself. His people revolted and put him to death in like manner.

Phaon, boatman of Mitylene, in Lesbos. Venus gave him a box of ointment when she appeared to him in the form of an old woman. When he applied the ointment to himself he became beautiful, and the famous poetess Sappho fell in love with him. He was devoted to her for a short time, but soon slighted her, on which she drowned herself in the sea.

Pharnabazus, satrap of Persia, who aided the Lacedaemonians against the Athenians, and gained their esteem by his devotion to their cause.

Pharos, small island in the bay of Alexandria, supporting a tower reputed to be one of the seven wonders of the world. Sostratus, son of Dexiphanes, built it in the reigns of Ptolemy Soter and Ptolemy Philadelphus.

Pharsalia, town of Thessaly famous for the great battle fought there, between Julius Caesar and Pompey, in which Caesar was victorious.

Pheasant, see Itys.

Phidias, famous sculptor of Athens, who carved a statue of Minerva, which was placed in the Pantheon. He died B.C. 432.

Philippi, Macedonian town, famous for two battles between Augustus and Antony, and the republican forces of Brutus and Cassius, in which the former were victorious.

Philippus, king of Macedonia, son of Amyntas. Epaminondas taught him the art of war. He wed Olympias, daughter of Neoptolemus, king of the Molossi, and became father of Alexander the Great. The battle of Chaeronea against the Greeks was fought during his reign, in which he was victorious. Philip was an artful and intriguing monarch but sagacious and prudent withal. Pausanias assassinated him during the wedding festivities of his daughter, B.C. 336. He was forty-seven years old, and had reigned twenty-four years.

Philippus, last king of Macedonia of that name, son of Demetrius. He wished for friendly relations with Hannibal. His intrigues were discovered by the Romans. They invaded his domain and Philip obtained peace, but only under very humiliating conditions. He died, B.C. 179, in the forty-second year of his reign.

Philo, Jewish writer of Alexandria, A.D. 40. He wrote on the laws, customs, and sacred history of the Jews, etc.

Philoctetes, one of the Argonauts to whom Hercules gave the arrows which had been dipped in the blood of the Hydra. In the tenth year of the Trojan war, the oracle informed the Greeks that Troy could not be taken without these arrows. Philoctetes took them to the Greek camp and destroyed Paris and a number of Trojans with their aid. Sophocles wrote one of his best tragedies on the adventures of Philoctetes.

Philomela, daughter of Pandion, king of Athens. Her sister Procne had married Tereus, king of Thrace. Procne, being separated from her sister, became very melancholy, and persuaded her husband to go to Athens and bring Philomela to Thrace. On the journey back Tereus treated Philomela with great cruelty, cutting off her tongue, and confining her in a lonely castle. He reported to Procne that she was dead, but Philomela found means of communicating with Procne, who, in revenge, murdered Tereus' son, and served him up as food at a banquet. When Tereus discovered this he drew his sword to kill the sisters, but he was changed into a hoopoe, Philomela into a nightingale, and Procne into a swallow.

Philopoemen, famous general of the Achaeans, born at Megalopolis. He was fond of rural life but early distinguished himself on the battlefield. He tried to model his career on that of Epaminondas, but lacked the prudence and other good qualities of the famous Theban. When Megalopolis was attacked by the Trojans, Philopoemen gave proof of his bravery. He became a commander, and with his own hands killed Mechanidas, the tyrant of Sparta, and defeated his army. With Sparta tributary to the Achaeans, Philopoemen had subdued one of the most powerful states of Greece. Eventually he was taken prisoner by the Messenians, and treated with great severity by their general. He died, 183 B.C., aged seventy, after having been poisoned.

Philostratus, famous Sophist, born either at Lemnos or Athens. He came to Rome, where he came under the patronage of the emperor's wife Julia. She gave him some papers concerning Apollonius, whose biography he wrote with elegance, but it contains exaggerations and improbable stories.

Phineus, son of Agenor, king of Phoenicia, or some state that he was son of Neptune. He became king of Thrace, and married Cleopatra, or Cleobula, daughter of Boreas. Plexippus and Pandion were their children. He married Idaea, after the death of Cleopatra. She was daughter of Dardanus, who, jealous of Cleopatra's children, accused them of attempting to kill their father, and they were condemned by Phineus to have their eyes put out. The gods punished this cruelty. Phineus was struck blind, and Jupiter sent the Harpies to keep him in continual alarm. He recovered his sight by means of the Argonauts, whom he had received hospitably.

Phlegethon, river in the infernal regions, where fire flowed between the banks instead of water. Nothing could grow on its parched and withered banks, and it presented a picture of desolation.

Phlegon, one of the freedmen of the emperor Adrian. He wrote a history of Sicily, and an account of the principal places in Rome, also treatises on other subjects. He was a poor stylist.

Phlegon, one of the four chariot horses of Sol, the name signifying "earth loving."

Phlegyas, son of Mars, and father of Ixion and Coronis. He was sent to Hades, and there compelled to sit with a huge stone suspended above his head, ready to be dropped at any moment. This was his punishment for desecrating and plundering the temple of Apollo at Delphi.

Phocion, distinguished Athenian famous for his zeal for the public good, and for military ability. The Athenians, losing sight of his virtues, accused him of treason, and he was condemned to drink poison, which he consumed with great heroism. He died about B.C. 318.

Phoebus, a name of Apollo, signifying light and life.

Phoenix, son of Amyntor, king of Argos, and Cleobule or Hippodamia; he was preceptor to Achilles. He went to the Trojan war with his pupil. He died in Thrace after the fall of Troy, and is said to have been buried near Trachinia, where a river was named after him.

Phryne, beautiful woman of Athens living about B.C. 328, who was beloved of Praxiteles, who painted her portrait. It is said that after Apelles had seen Phryne on the sea-shore with dishevelled hair, he was inspired to paint his Venus Anadyomene. Another of the same name was accused of impiety. When the judges were about to condemn her she bared her bosom, and her beauty so captivated them that they acquitted her.

Phryxus, son of Athamas, king of Thebes, and Nephele. He divorced Nephele on a plea of her insanity. He then married Ino, who persecuted Phryxus because he was to succeed to the throne in preference to one of her own children. Realising that Ino had designs on his life, he and his sister Helle started to go to Aetes, king of Colchis. They mounted a ram, with a golden fleece, whoch rose in the air, and steered a course for Colchis. Helle, becoming giddy, fell into the sea, afterwards called Helles-pont. Phryxus arrived at the court of Aetes, and married his daughter Chalciope. Later he was killed by his father-in-law. His murder gave rise to the famous Argonautic expedition under Jason, whose object was to recover the Golden Fleece.

Phyllis, daughter of Sithon, or some writers say Lycurgus, king of Thrace. Demophon landed on her coasts on his return from the Trojan wars, and they fell in love. Later, Demophon proving faithless, Phyllis hanged herself. Tradition says she was changed into an almond tree.

Picus, king of Latium, son of Saturn, who married Vanilia. He was met by Circe while out hunting. She became enamoured with him and changed him into a woodpecker.

Pierides, a name of the Muses from Pieria, where they were born. Also the daughters of Pierus, king of Macedonia, who settled in Boeotia. They challenged the Muses to sing, and were changed into magpies.

Pillar, see Calpe.

Pilumnus, rural divinity, presiding over corn whilst it was being ground.

Pindarus, famous lyric poet of Thebes. When young it was said that a swarm of bees settled on his lips, leaving on them some honey, which was regarded as a sign of his future greatness. Great respect was shown to his memory after his death; a statue was erected to his honour in the most public place in Thebes. He is said to have died, B.C. 435, aged eighty-six. Only his odes remain.

Pine-tree, see Atys.

Piraeus, famous harbour at Athens, some three miles from the city. It was connected with the town by two walls, one built by Pericles, and the other by Themistocles.

Pirithous, son of Ixion and Dia, the daughter of Deioneus. He was king of the Lapithae, who became a cordial friend of Theseus, king of Athens. He married Hippodamia, and invited the Centaurs to the wedding. They became intoxicated and behaved rudely, upon which they were attacked and overcome by Theseus, Pirithous, Hercules and the rest of the Lapithae. Many of the Centaurs were killed, and the rest were put to flight.

Pisander, commander of the Spartan fleet during the Peloponnesian war. He was against democracy. He was killed in battle at sea near Cnidus, B.C. 394.

Pisistratus, famous Athenian distinguished for valour in the field and eloquence at home. He had a bodyguard of fifty to defend his person. With these he seized the citadel of Athens, soon making himself absolute ruler. A conspiracy was formed against him and he was banished from the city. He soon re-established himself in power, and married the daughter of Megacles, one of his greatest enemies. His popularity then waned and he fled from Athens. Returning eleven years later, he was received with acclamation. He died about B.C. 527.

Piso, famous Roman family, no less than eleven of whom became consuls, and some were honoured with triumphs for their victories. The most famous were—Lucius Calpurnius, who was tribune about B.C. 149, and later consul. He was an orator, statesman, and historian. Caius, who was firm during his consulship in resisting the tumults raised by the tribunes. Cneius, a consul under Augustus who was notorious for cruelty. Lucius, a governor of

Spain, who was murdered by a peasant. Lucius, a governor of Rome for twenty years, a man moderate and just. Caius, who headed a conspiracy against Nero. He committed suicide.

Pitho, goddess of persuasion, daughter of Mercury and Venus; she was sometimes called Suada.

Pittacus, one of the seven wise men of Greece, born at Mitylene in Lesbos. His maxims were inscribed on the walls of Apollo's temple at Delphi, showing the high opinion in which he was held by his countrymen. He spent the latter part of his life in retirement. He died, B.C. 570, aged eighty-two.

Plancus, L. Munatius, Roman noted for extravagance and folly. He had held high offices in the state, but forgetting his dignity became a servile flatterer of Antony and Cleopatra.

Plants, see Demogorgon.

Plataea, town of Boeotia, near Mt. Citheron, noted for a battle between Mardonius, a general of Xerxes, and Pausanias, commanding the Athenians. The Persians suffered a great defeat.

Plato, famous Athenian philosopher. His education was carefully arranged and his body developed by gymnastic exercises. He started his career by writing poetry and tragedies. When he was twenty he was introduced to Socrates, whose pupil he became. He travelled abroad in several countries, eventually settling near Athens, where his lectures were attended by a crowd of illustrious pupils. His writings were so famous, and his opinions so highly esteemed, that he was called the Divine. He died, B.C. 348, aged eighty-one.

Plautus, M. Accius, dramatic poet born in Umbria. Nineteen of his twenty-five comedies remain. He died B.C. 184.

Pleasure, see Rembha.

Pleiades, name given to the seven daughters of Atlas and Pleione. Their names were Alcyone, Celaeno, Electra, Maia, Merope, Sterope, and Taygete. After death they were placed in the heavens as a constellation, but only six stars are seen. The ancients believed that Merope married a mortal, and was ashamed to show herself among her sisters who all married gods.

Plinius, C. Secundus, called the Elder, was born at Verona, of noble blood. He was made governor of Spain. When in command of the Roman fleet at Misenum, Pliny saw the appearance of a cloud of dust and ashes, which was the opening of the famous eruption of Mt. Vesuvius which buried Herculaneum and Pompeii. Sailing to the scene he was suffocated by the vapours. This happened A.D. 79.

Plinius, C. Caecilius Secundus, called Pliny the Younger. He was son of L. Caecilius by the sister of Pliny the Elder. At nineteen he had already distinguished himself at the bar. When Trajan became emperor, Pliny was created consul. He had a great deal to do with the persecution of the Christians, and wrote a now famous letter to Trajan, asking for instructions as to how to deal with Christians when they appeared before him. He died, A.D. 113, aged fifty-two.

Plutarchus, famous biographer, born at Chaeronea, whose father was distinguished for virtue and learning. After travelling in quest of knowledge he retired to Rome, opening a school there. Later he went to Chaeronea, where he died in advanced years, A.D. 140. His best known work is his "Lives of Illustrious Men."

Pluto, son of Saturn and Ops, inherited his father's kingdom with his brothers, Jupiter and Neptune. His portion was the infernal regions. He seized Proserpine as she gathered flowers in the meadows, and carried her away in his chariot, married her, making her queen of the infernal regions. His principal attendant was a three-headed dog named Cerberus, and about his throne were the Eumenides, the Harpies, and the Furies. He is sometimes referred to as Dis.

Plutus, god of riches, son of Jason and Ceres. He was reputed to be blind and lame; blind because he so often injudiciously bestows his riches, and lame because fortunes come so slowly.

Pluvius, a name of Jupiter, because he controlled the rain.

Podalirius, son of Aesculapius, a famous surgeon who worked amongst the soldiers in the Trojan war.

Poet, see Parnassus.

Poetry, see Apollo, Calliope, the Muses.

Poisonous herbs, see Circe.

Poisonous lake, see Avernus.

Pollear, son of Siva, the Hindoo god of wisdom.

Pollux, son of Jupiter and Leda, and twin brother of Castor. The brothers form the constellation of Gemini. The Greeks called him Polydeuces. See Aedepol.

Polybotes, one of the giants who made war against Jupiter.

Polydectes, son of Magnes, king of Seriphus. When Danae and her son Perseus had been exposed on the sea, he received them kindly. Polydectes was turned to stone when shown Medusa's head by Perseus.

Polyhymnia, daughter of Jupiter and Mnemosyne, the Muse presiding over singing and rhetoric.

Polynices, son of Oedipus, king of Thebes, and Jocasta. He and his brother Eteocles succeeded their father and agreed to reign in alternate years. Eteocles ascended the throne first, and refused to resign the crown. Polynices fled to Argos, and married Argia, daughter of Adrastus, king of Argos; he raised an army and marched on Thebes. The two brothers decided the battle in single combat; both were killed.

Polyphemus, most famous of the Cyclopes, son of Neptune and Thoosa, daughter of Phorcys. He captured Ulysses and twelve of his companions, and is said to have eaten six of them. The rest were rescued by Ulysses, who put out the monster's single eye with a firebrand.

Polyxena, daughter of Priam, king of Troy; by her treachery Achilles was shot in the heel.

Pomona, nymph at Rome presiding over gardens and fruit trees.

Pompeii, or Pompeium, town of Campania, partly destroyed by an earthquake, A.D. 63, and sixteen years later overwhelmed by another earthquake, together with Herculaneum.

Pompeius, Cneius, surnamed Magnus for his exploits. He espoused the cause of Sylla against Marius. Later he united his interest with that of Caesar and Crassus, so forming the first triumvirate. They soon disagreed and at the battle of Pharsalia, where Caesar's forces met those of Pompey, the latter was defeated, and fled to Egypt, where he was assassinated, B.C. 48, aged fifty-eight. His two sons, Cneius and Sextus, were masters of a powerful army with which they attacked Caesar, but were defeated in the battle of Manda, where Cneius was killed. Sextus escaped, but was put to death by Antony about B.C. 35.

Poplar-tree, see Heliades.

Porcia, daughter of Cato of Utica, who married Bibulus, and after his death, Brutus. She was known to be prudent and courageous. When her husband died she destroyed herself by swallowing burning coals.

Porphyrius, Platonic philosopher of Tyre, who studied eloquence at Athens under Longinus, and later retired to Rome. His best work referred to the Christian religion. Porphyry died, A.D. 304, aged seventy-one.

Porsenna, or Porsena, king of Etruria, who declared war on Rome because of the refusal to restore Tarquin to the throne. He was prevented from entering the gates of Rome by P. Horatius Cocles, who standing at the head of a bridge kept back the army, whilst the bridge was destroyed by the Romans. Later Porsenna abandoned the cause of Tarquin.

Portunus, son of Ino, was god of harbours.

Poseidon, a name of Neptune.

Pracriti, Hindoo goddess of nature.

Praxiteles, famous Grecian sculptor, whose statue of Cupid he gave to Phryne. He flourished about B.C. 324.

Priamus, last king of Troy, son of Laomedon, by Strymo, or some state Placia. His wife was Arisba, whom he divorced to marry Hecuba. They had a number of children including Hector, Deiphobus, Helenus, Laodice, and Cassandra. Hercules had carried off Priam's sister Heisone, and, being anxious to recover her, he manned a fleet, and sent his son Paris to fetch her. Instead of obeying his father's instructions, he carried away Helen, wife of Menelaus, king of Sparta. This gave rise to the Trojan war which lasted for ten years. At the end of the war, Neoptolemus, son of Achilles, slew Priam.

Priapus, god of natural reproduction, and guardian of gardens. He was son of Venus and Bacchus.

Prisca, a name of Vesta.

Probus, M. Aurelius, was born at Pannonia. His father had been a gardener, who became tribune. His son also became tribune at the age of twenty-two, distinguishing himself for probity and valour. He was elected emperor, adding glories to his country by his victories. He was slain by his soldiers, B.C. 282, aged fifty.

Procne, wife of Tereus. See Itys and Tereus.

Procopius, a relative of the emperor Julian, who was born of a noble family in Cilicia. Under Julian he became distinguished, later retiring to the Thracian Chersonesus, whence he appeared in Constantinople, proclaiming himself master of the Eastern Empire. He was defeated in Phrygia, and beheaded, B.C. 366. Another of the same name was a famous Greek historian, who wrote a history of the reign of Justinian, and who was secretary to Belisarius.

Procris, daughter of the king of Athens. See Cephalus.

Prometheus, son of Japetes and Clymene, and father of Deucalion. He ridiculed the gods and displeased Jupiter by making clay figures and animating them with fire he had stolen from heaven. To punish him and the rest of mankind, Jupiter took fire away from the earth. With the assistance of Minerva, Prometheus climbed to heaven, and stole fire from the chariot of the sun, bringing it down to earth. This so provoked Jupiter that he ordered Prometheus to be chained to a rock on Mt. Caucasus, where a vulture preyed daily on his liver, which grew at night as much as it had been reduced during the day. He was delivered by Hercules, who killed the vulture.

Propertius, Sextus Aurelius, poet born in Umbria, who came to Rome where his genius recommended him to the great and powerful. He wrote four books of elegies. He died B.C. 19.

Prophecy, see Nereus.

Proserpina, daughter of Jupiter and Ceres, called Persephone by the Greeks. Pluto carried her off to the infernal regions whilst she was gathering flowers, and married her. Ceres, on learning this, demanded of Jupiter that Pluto should be punished. As queen of hell, Proserpine presided over the death of mankind. She was also known as Libitina, Inferna, Juno, Hecate, etc.

Protagoras, Greek philosopher of Abdera in Thrace, who wrote a book denying the existence of a Supreme Being. The book was publicly burned at Athens, and its author banished.

Protesilaus, king of part of Thessaly. He married Laodamia, soon repairing to the Trojan war. He was the first Greek to enter the Trojan domain. On this account, according to the prediction of the oracle, he was killed by his countrymen.

Proteus, sea deity, son of Oceanus and Tethys, or, some state, Neptune and Phenice. He received the gift of prophecy from Neptune. He sometimes escaped the importunities of those who came to consult him by assuming various shapes.

Psyche, nymph whom Cupid married. For this Venus put her to death, but, at Cupid's request, Jupiter granted her immortality.

Ptolemae, Ptolemacus First, surnamed Lagus, was king of Egypt, and son of Arsinoe and Lagus. He was brought up at the court of the king of Macedonia, and when Alexander invaded Asia, Ptolemy attended him. At the death of Alexander, Ptolemy secured the government of Egypt, gaining the esteem of the people. He became master of Phoenicia and Syria, and gave assistance to the people of Rhodes against their enemies, for which he received the name Soter. He founded a library which became the most famous in the world. He died, B.C. 284, aged eighty-four. His son, Ptolemy Philadelphus, proved his worthy successor. His palace became the resort of the learned, and he greatly added to the library his father had founded. Ptolemy the Third followed his father Philadelphus. He subdued Syria and Cilicia, returning laden with spoils. He also patronised the arts. The fourth Ptolemy was called Philopater, who proved to be cruel and oppressive. He died, B.C. 204, aged thirty-seven, after reigning seventeen years. Others of the family who succeeded did not approach the greatness of the founders.

Ptolemaeus, famous geographer and astronomer in the reign of Adrian and Antoninus.

Publicola, surname, signifying a friend of the commonalty, acquired by Publius Valerius. He helped Brutus to expel the Tarquins. He was four times consul, but dying in poverty, was buried at the public expense, amidst general mourning.

Pygmalion, famous sculptor, who had adopted celibacy, but made such a beautiful model of a goddess that he begged Venus to give it life. He married the animated statue.

Pylotis, a Greek name of Minerva.

Pyracmon, one of the chiefs of the Cyclopes.

Pyrois, one of the four chariot-horses of Sol, signifying luminous.

Pyrrhus, king of Epirus, son of Aeacides and Phthia, who wrote several books on encampments and army training. He fought against the Romans with great courage and was praised by them. He was killed in an attack on Argos, by a tile thrown on his head from a housetop.

Pyrrhus, see Neoptolemus.

Pythagoras, famous philosopher born at Samos. When eighteen years of age he gained the prize for wrestling at the Olympic games. He made discoveries in astronomy, mathematics, and geometry, and he was first to subscribe to the doctrine of transmigration of the soul. He taught that the universe was a shapeless mass of passive matter in the hands of a powerful Being, who was mover and soul of the world, and of whose substance the souls of mankind were a portion. He is said by some to have died at Metapontum, B.C. 497, but the place of his death is not definitely known.

Pythia, priestess of Apollo at Delphi, who delivered the answers of the oracle. The name is also applied to the games held in honour of Apollo's victory over the Python.

Python, famous serpent which sprang from the mud and stagnant waters after the deluge of Deucalion. The monster was slain by Apollo. See Septerion.

Q

Quadratus, surname given to Mercury, because some of his statues were four-sided.

Quadrifrons, Janus was sometimes depicted with four faces instead of two, when he was known as Janus Quadrifrons.

Quies, Roman goddess of rest; her temple was just outside the Collini gate of Rome.

Quietus, a name of Pluto.

Quintilianus Marcus Fabius, famous rhetorician, born in Spain, who opened a school of rhetoric in Rome and was the first salaried state teacher. He died A.D. 95.

Quintus Curtius Rufus, Latin historian said to have lived in the reign of Vespasian. He wrote the history of the reign of Alexander the Great.

Quirinus, name given to Mars in times of war. Virgil refers to Jupiter under the same name.

Quoit, see Hyacinthus.

R

Race, see Atalanta.

Radamanthus, see Rhadamanthus.

Rage, see Furies.

Rainbow, see Iris.

Rama, Hindoo god, terrestrial representation of Vishnu.

Ram's hide, see Golden Fleece.

Reeds, see Pan and Syrinx.

Regillus, small lake in Latium, which was the scene of the Roman victory in the Battle of Lake Regillus.

Regulus, M. Attilius, was consul during the first Punic war. He reduced Brundusium, and later captured the bulk of the Carthaginian fleet. Finally he was taken prisoner and tortured to death by the Carthaginians.

Rembha, Hindoo goddess of pleasure.

Reproduction, see Priapus.

Rest, see Quies.

Revenge, see Ate.

Rhadamanthus, son of Jupiter and Europa, was judge of the Asiatics in the infernal regions.

Rhamnusia, a name of Nemesis, from Rhamnus, a town in Attica, where she had a temple containing her statue, fashioned from one stone, ten cubits high.

Rhea, Greek name of Cybele.

Rhetoric, see Calliope, Polyhymnia.

Riches, see Plutus.

Rimmon, one of the Phrygian gods.

Riot, see Saturnalia.

River of fire, see Phlegethon.

Roads, see Vialis.

Robber, see Cacus, Coeculus.

Romulus, traditional founder of Rome; son of Mars and Ilia, and twin brother of Remus. The infants were thrown into the Tiber, but were saved and suckled by a she-wolf till found by Faustulus, a shepherd, who brought them up. Remus was slain in a dispute with his brother, and Romulus became the famous emperor.

Roscius, famous Roman actor. He died about 60 B.C.

Rubicon, small river in Italy. Caesar crossed it, thus transgressing the boundaries of his province and declaring war on the senate and Pompey. "Passing the Rubicon" has become a proverbial indication of an irrevocable step taken in any weighty matter.

Rumia Dea, Roman goddess of babes in arms.

Runcia, goddess of weeding and cleansing the ground.

S

Sacra Via, important street in Rome, where a treaty of peace was made between Romulus and Tatius.

Sacrifices, ceremonious offerings made to the gods. A distinct victim was allotted to each deity, and the greatest care taken of their selection, as any blemish was an insult to the god. At the time of sacrifice the people were called together by heralds led by a procession of musicians. The priest wore white robes and was crowned with a wreath of the leaves of the tree which was sacred to the god to whom the sacrifice was being offered. The victim was adorned with a similar chaplet and had its horns gilded, and was decorated with brightly coloured ribbons. The priest would enquire, "Who is here?" to which the congregation replied, "Many good people." Then the priest would say, "Begone all ye who are profane," and start a prayer addressed to all the gods. The sacrifice commenced by putting corn, frankincense, flour, salt, cakes and fruit on the head of the victim. This was known as the Immolation. The priest then took a cup of wine, tasted it, and handed it to the bystanders to taste also. Some of it was then poured between the horns of the victim, and a few saturated hairs were pulled off and placed in the fire burning on the altar. Turning to the east, the priest drew a crooked line down the back of the beast with his knife, telling the assistants to kill the animal. The entrails were then removed and examined by the Aruspices to find out what was prognosticated. The carcass was then divided, and the thighs, covered with fat, were put in the fire, and the remainder cut up, cooked, and eaten. This feast was celebrated with music and dancing, and hymns in praise of the god in whose honour the sacrifice was made. On great occasions hundreds of bullocks were offered at one time. It is said that Pythagoras made such an offering when he discovered the demonstration of the forty-seventh proposition of the book of Euclid.

Saga, Scandinavian goddess of history.

Saggitarius, see Chiron.

Sails, see Daedalus.

Salamanders, genii who, according to Plato, lived in fire.

Salamis, island of Attica famous for a battle fought there between the Greek and Persian fleets, in which the latter suffered defeat.

Salatia, see Amphitrite.

Salii, priests of Mars who had custody of the sacred shields.

Sallustius, Crispus, famous Latin historian. He wrote a history of the Catilinian conspiracy; he died 35 B.C.

Salmoneus, king of Elis, who for trying to imitate the splendours of Jupiter was sent straight to the infernal regions by the god.

Salus, Roman god of health.

Sanchoniathon, Phoenician historian born at Berytus, or, some say, Tyre. He lived a few years before the Trojan war, and wrote on the antiquities of Phoenicia.

Sapor, king of Persia who came to the throne about 238 A.D. He endeavoured to increase his domains by conquest, but was defeated by Odenatus. He was assassinated A.D. 273.

Sapor, second king of Persia by that name. He fought against the Romans, gaining several victories. He died A.D. 380.

Sappho, famous for beauty and poetical talents. She was born at Lesbos about 600 B.C. She became enamoured with Phaon, a youth of Mitylene. He did not return her regard, and in consequence she threw herself into the sea from the rock of Leucadia.

Sarcasm, see Momus.

Sardanapalus, last king of Assyria, famous for luxury and indolence. His subjects conspired against him with success, on which he fired his palace and perished in the flames, B.C. 820.

Saron, a sea-god.

Saturnalia, festivals held in honour of Saturn in mid-December.

They were famous for riotous disorder.

Saturnius, name given to Jupiter, Neptune, and Pluto, as sons of Saturn.

Saturnus, son of Coelus, or Uranus, by Terra. Human sacrifices were offered at his altar until the custom was abolished by Hercules. He is represented as an old man bent with age, carrying a scythe in his right hand.

Satyavrata, Hindoo god of law. The same as Menu.

Satyrs, attendants of Silenus, similar to the fauns who attended Pan. See Silenus.

Scaevola, Mucius, surnamed Cordus, famous for courage. He attempted to assassinate Porsenna, but was seized. To show his fortitude when confronted with Porsenna, he thrust his hand into the fire, upon which the king pardoned him.

Scipio, name of a famous Roman family, the most conspicuous of which was Publius Cornelius, afterwards called Africanus. He was son of Publius Scipio, and commanded an army against the Carthaginians. After gaining some victories he encountered Hannibal at the famous battle of Zama, in which he obtained a decisive victory. He died 184 B.C., aged 48.

Scipio, Lucius Cornelius, surnamed Asiaticus, accompanied his brother Africanus in his expedition to Africa. He was made consul A.U.C. 562, and sent to attack Antiochus, king of Syria, whom he subdued. He was accused of receiving bribes from Antiochus, and was condemned to pay large fines, which reduced him to poverty.

Scipio, P. Aemilianus, called Africanus the Younger. He completed the war with Carthage, B.C. 147. The city was set on fire, and Scipio is said to have wept bitterly over the melancholy scene. On his return to Rome he was sent to conclude the war against Numantia, which he did with success, and added Numantinus to his name. He was discovered dead in bed, and was presumed to have been strangled, B.C. 128.

Scylla, beautiful nymph who excited the jealousy of Neptune's wife, Amphitrite, who turned her into a frightful sea-monster, with six fearsome heads and necks. Rising unexpectedly from the

sea she would take as many as six sailors from a ship, and carry
them to the bottom of the sea. An alternative danger with Charybdis.

Scylla, daughter of Nysus, who was changed into a lark for cutting off a charmed lock of her father's hair. See Nysus.

Sea, see Neptune.

Seasons, see Vertumnus.

Sea-weed, see Glaucus.

Segesta, rural divinity who protected corn during harvest.

Sem, the Egyptian Hercules.

Semi-Dei, the demi-gods.

Semiramis, famous queen of Assyria, who married the governor
of Nineveh, and after his death, King Ninus. She improved
her kingdom, and distinguished herself as a warrior. She is said to
have lived around 1965 B.C.

Semones, Roman gods of a class between "immortal" and the
"mortal," such as satyrs and fauns.

Seneca, L. Annaeus, preceptor to Nero, who later determined
to put him to death. Seneca chose to have his veins opened in a
hot bath, but death not ensuing, he swallowed poison, and was
eventually suffocated by the soldiers in attendance. He wrote
many works, chiefly on moral subjects. He died 56 A.D., aged
fifty-three.

Septerion, festival in honour of Apollo, at which his victory
over Python was grandly represented.

Serapis, the Egyptian Jupiter, supposed to be the same as Osiris.
He had magnificent temples at Memphis, Alexandria, and Canopus.

Serpent, Greeks and Romans considered the serpent symbolical
of guardian spirits, and as such were often engraved on their
altars. See Aesculapius, Apollo, Chimera, Eurydice, and Medusa.

Seshanaga, the Egyptian Pluto.

Sesostris, famous king of Egypt, living long before the Trojan
war. He achieved many conquests, and encouraged the fine arts.
He committed suicide after a reign of forty-four years.

Severus, Lucius Septimius, Roman emperor, born in Africa. He

invaded Britain, and built a wall in the north to check the incur-
sions of the Caledonians. He died at York, A.D. 211.

Sewers, see Cloacina.

Sharp-sightedness, see Lynceus.

Shepherds, see Pan.

Shields, see Ancilia.

Ships, see Neptune.

Silence, see Harpocrates and Tacita.

Silenus, Bacchanalian demi-god, chief of the Satyrs. He is represented as a fat, drunken old man, riding on an ass, crowned with
flowers.

Silius Italicus, C., Latin poet who retired from the bar to study.
He imitated Virgil, but with little success. His poetry is, however,
commended for its purity.

Simonides, famous poet of Ceos who lived around B.C. 538. He
wrote elegies, epigrams, and drama, esteemed for beauty.

Singing, see Polyhymnia, Thanyris.

Sirenes, the Sirens, who lured to destruction those who listened
to their songs. When Ulysses sailed past their island he stopped
the ears of his companions with wax, and had himself bound to
the mast of the ship. So he passed safely, and the Sirens, disap-
pointed of their prey, drowned themselves.

Sisyphus, son of Aeolus and Enaretta. After death he was condemned to roll a stone, in the infernal regions, to the top of a
hill, which always rolled back, rendering his punishment eternal.

Siva, in Hindoo mythology, the "changer of form."

Slaughter, see Furies.

Slaves, see Feronia.

Sleep, see Caduceus, Morpheus, and Somnus.

Sleipner, eight-legged horse of Odin, chief of the Scandinavian
gods.

Socrates, most famous philosopher of antiquity, born near
Athens, whose virtues rendered his name venerable. His independence of spirit gained him many enemies, and he was accused of
making innovations in the religion of the Greeks. He was condemned to death by drinking hemlock, and expired a few mo-

ments after drinking the poison. His wife was Xanthippe, of shrewish disposition, for which her name has become proverbial. Socrates died B.C. 400, aged seventy.

Sol, the sun. The worship of the god Sol is the oldest on record, and although he is sometimes referred to as being the same as Apollo, there is no doubt he was worshipped by the Egyptians, Persians and others long before the Apollo of the Greeks was heard of. See Surya.

Solon, one of the wise men of Greece, born at Salamis, and educated at Athens. After travelling over Greece he was elected archon and sovereign legislator. He effected numerous reforms, binding the Athenians by a solemn oath to observe the laws he enacted for one hundred years. Later he visited Egypt, and returning after ten years' absence, he found most of his regulations disregarded. On this he retired to Cyprus, where he died 558 B.C., aged eighty.

Somnus, son of Nox and Erebus, was one of the infernal deities. He presided over sleep, and lived in a gloomy cave, void of light and air.

Sophocles, famous tragic poet of Athens. He was also a statesman who held the office of Archon. He wrote drama and won the poetical prize on twenty occasions. He rivalled Euripides in public opinion. He died B.C. 406, aged ninety-one.

Sophonisba, daughter of Hasdrubal, the Carthaginian, famous for her beauty. She married Syphax, prince of Numidia; when he was conquered by the Romans she became a captive to their ally, the Numidian general Masinissa, whom she married. This angered the Romans, and Scipio ordered Masinissa to separate from Sophonisba; urged by Masinissa she took poison and died about B.C. 203.

Sospita, a name of Juno, as the safeguard of women.

Soter, Greek name of Jupiter, signifying deliverer.

Soul, see Psyche.

South wind, see Auster.

Spear, see Pelias.

Sphinx, a monster, having the head and breasts of a woman, the body of a dog, the tail of a serpent, the wings of a bird, and the paws of a lion. The Sphinx was sent into the neighbourhood of Thebes by Juno, where she propounded enigmas, devouring those unable to solve them. One of the riddles proposed was: What animal walked on four legs in the morning, two at noon, and three in the evening? Oedipus solved it, giving as the meaning: A man, who when an infant crawled on his hands and feet, walking erect in manhood, and in the evening of life supporting himself with a stick. On hearing the solution the Sphinx destroyed herself.

Spider, see Arachne.

Spindle, see Pallas.

Spinning, see Arachne, Ergotis.

Spring, see Vertumnus.

Stable, see Augaeas.

Stagira, town on the borders of Macedonia, where Aristotle was born. Hence he is called the Stagirite.

Stars, see Aurora.

Statius, P. Papinius, poet born at Naples in the time of Domitian. He wrote two epic poems, the Thebais in twelve books, and the Achilleis in two books.

Stentor, one of the Greeks who went to the Trojan war, noted for his strength of voice; from him the term "stentorian" has become proverbial.

Sterentius, Roman god who invented the art of manuring lands. See also Picumnus.

Steropes, one of the Cyclopes.

Stoici, famous sect of philosophers founded by Zeno. They preferred virtue to all things, regarding all opposed to it as evil.

Stone, see Medusa, Phlegyas.

Stone, rolling, see Sisyphus.

Strabo, famous geographer, born at Amasia, on the borders of Cappadocia. He lived in the time of Augustus. His geographical work consists of seventeen books, and is admired for its clarity.

Streets, see Apollo.

Stymphalides, carnivorous birds destroyed in the sixth labour of Hercules.

Styx, famous river of the infernal regions, held in such high esteem that the gods always swore "by the Styx," such an oath never being violated. See Achilles, Thetis.

Suada, goddess of persuasion. See Pitho.

Success, see Bonus Eventus.

Suetonius, C. Tranquillus, Latin historian who became secretary to Adrian. He wrote the Lives of the Caesars.

Sulla, see Sylla.

Sun, see Aurora, Belus, Sol, Surya.

Sunflower, see Clytie.

Suradevi, Hindoo goddess of wine.

Surgeon, see Podalirius.

Surya, Hindoo god corresponding to the Roman Sol, the sun.

Swallow, see Itys.

Swan, see Cygnus, Leda.

Swiftness, see Atalanta.

Swine, see Circe.

Sybaris, town on the Bay of Tarentum. The inhabitants were noted for their love of ease and pleasure, hence the term "sybarite."

Sylla (or Sulla), L. Cornelius, famous Roman of noble blood, conspicuous in military affairs, who became antagonistic to Marius. In the zenith of his power he was guilty of great cruelty. He died B.C. 70, aged sixty.

Sylphs, genii who, according to Plato, lived in the air.

Sylvester, name of Mars when he was invoked to protect cultivated land from the ravages of war.

Syphax, king of Masaesyllii in Numidia, who married Sophonisba, daughter of Hasdrubal. He joined the Carthaginians against the Romans, and was taken by Scipio as a prisoner to Rome, where he died in prison.

Syrinx, name of the nymph who, to escape from the importunities of Pan, was changed by Diana into reeds, out of which he made his famous pipes, naming them "the Syrinx."

T

Tacita, goddess of silence. See Harpocrates.

Tacitus, C. Cornelius, famous Latin historian, born in the reign of Nero. The "Annals" is the most complete and extensive of his works. He wrote forcefully and with precision and dignity, his Latin being pure and classical.

Tantalus, father of Niobe and Pelops, who as a punishment for serving up his son Pelops as meat at a feast to the gods, was placed in a pool in the infernal regions. Whenever he attempted to quench his burning thirst the waters receded. Hence the term "tantalising."

Tarquinius Priscus, fifth king of Rome, son of Demaratus, a native of Greece. He gained victories over the Sabines. During peace he turned his attention to the improvement of the capital. He was assassinated B.C. 578, aged eighty.

Tarquinius Superbus, ascended the throne after Servius Tullius, whom he murdered, and married his daughter Tullia. He was a tyrant and was eventually expelled from Rome. He died in his ninetieth year.

Tartarus, an inner region of hell, where, according to Virgil, the gods sent the souls of those who were exceptionally depraved for punishment.

Telchines, priests of Cybele, who were famous magicians.

Telemachus, son of Penelope and Ulysses. He went in search of his father at the end of the Trojan war, finding him with the aid of Minerva. Assisted by Ulysses he delivered his mother from the suitors who beset her.

Tempe, a valley in Thessaly, through which the river Peneus flows into the Aegean Sea. The poets describe it as one of the most delightful places in the world.

Tempests, see Fro.

Temple, edifice erected to the honour of a god or goddess, to which the sacrifices were offered.

Tenth Muse, Sappho was so called.

Terentius, Publius (Terence), a native of Africa famous for the comedies he wrote. His first play was produced in Rome when he was twenty-five years old. He is thought to have been drowned in a storm about B.C. 159.

Tereus, son of Mars. He married Procne, daughter of Pandion, king of Athens, but fell in love with her sister Philomela, who resented his attentions, which so enraged him that he cut out her tongue. When Procne heard of her husband's unfaithfulness she took a terrible revenge (see Itys). Procne was turned into a swallow, Philomela into a nightingale, Itys into a hoopoe, a kind of vulture, some say an owl.

Tergemina, a name of Diana, alluding to her triform divinity as goddess of heaven, earth, and hell.

Terminus, Roman god of boundaries.

Terpsichore, one of the Muses, daughter of Jupiter and Mnemosyne. She presided over dancing.

Terra, the earth, one of the most ancient Greek goddesses.

Tertullianus, J. Septimius Florens, famous Christian writer of Carthage who lived A.D. 196. Originally a pagan, he became an able advocate of Christianity.

Thais, famous woman of Athens, who accompanied Alexander the Great in his Asiatic conquests.

Thales, one of the seven wise men of Greece, born at Miletus in Ionia. He made great discoveries in astronomy, and was first to calculate with accuracy a solar eclipse. He died about 548 B.C.

Thalestris, queen of the Amazons.

Thalia, one of the Muses, presiding over festivals and comedy.

Thanyris, presumed to challenge the Muses to sing, on condition that if he did not sing best they might inflict any penalty they pleased. He was defeated and punished with blindness.

Theia, daughter of Coelus and Terra, wife of Hyperion.

Themis, daughter of Coelus and Terra, and wife of Jupiter, was Roman goddess of laws, ceremonies, and oracles.

Themistocles, famous general born at Athens. When Xerxes invaded Greece, Themistocles was given the care of the fleet, and at the battle of Salamis, B.C. 480, the Greeks, instigated to fight by Themistocles, obtained the victory over the navy of Xerxes. He died aged sixty-five, some say poisoned by drinking bull's blood.

Theocritus, Greek poet who lived at Syracuse in Sicily 282 B.C.

Theodosius, Flavius, Roman emperor surnamed Magnus from the greatness of his exploits. Early in his reign he conquered the Barbarians. He lived a temperate life and reigned sixteen years. He died A.D. 395, aged sixty.

Theodosius the Second, became emperor of the West at an early age. The Persians invaded his territories, but on his appearance at the head of a large force they fled, losing many men in the Euphrates. Theodosius was a warm advocate of the Christian religion. He died A.D. 450, aged forty-nine.

Theophrastus, a native of Lesbos. Diogenes enumerates the titles of more than two hundred treatises which he wrote. He died B.C. 288, aged 107.

Thermopylae, narrow pass leading from Thessaly into Phocis, famous for the battle fought there, B.C. 480, between Xerxes and the Greeks, in which three hundred Spartans, led by Leonidas, resisted for three days an enormous Persian army.

Thersites, a deformed Greek in the Trojan war, who ridiculed Ulysses and others. Achilles killed him because he laughed at his grief for the death of Penthesilea.

Theseus, king of Athens, and son of Aegeus by Aethra, was one of the most famous heroes of antiquity. He caught the bull of Marathon and sacrificed it to Minerva. He went to Crete amongst the seven youths sent yearly by the Athenians to be devoured by the Minotaur, and with the aid of Ariadne he slew the monster. He ascended his father's throne B.C. 1235. Pirithous, king of Lapithae, invaded his territories, but the two became firm friends. They went to the infernal regions to rescue Proserpine, but were frustrated by Pluto. After remaining some time in the infernal regions, Theseus returned to his kingdom to find his throne filled by an usurper, whom he vainly tried to eject. He retired to Scyros, where he was killed by a fall from a precipice.

Thesmorphonius, a name of Ceres.

Thespis, Greek poet of Attica, supposed to be the inventor of tragedy, B.C. 536. He went from place to place upon a cart, from which he gave performances. Hence the term "thespians" as applied to travelling actors.

Thetis, sea-goddess, daughter of Nereus and Doris. She married Peleus, king of Thessaly, and became mother of Achilles, whom she plunged into the Styx, thus rendering him invulnerable in every part of his body except the heel by which she held him. See Achilles.

Thief, see Laverna, Mercury.

Thisbe, beautiful maiden of Babylon beloved by Pyramus.

Thor, Scandinavian god of war, son of Odin, who ruled the aerial regions, and, like Jupiter, hurled thunder against his foes.

Thor's Belt, a girdle which doubled the god's strength each time he put it on.

Thoth, the Mercury of the Egyptians.

Thrasybulus, famous general of Athens, who, with the help of a few associates, expelled the thirty tyrants, B.C. 401. He was given a powerful fleet to recover the Athenian power on the coast of Asia. After many victories he was killed by the people of Aspendus.

Thucidydes, famous Greek historian, born at Athens. He wrote the history of the Peloponnesian war. He died 391 B.C., aged eighty.

Thunderbolts, see Cyclops.

Thunderer, The, Jupiter. See Tonitrualis.

Thya, a name of Ops.

Thyades, priestesses of Bacchus, who ran wild in the hills, wearing tiger-skins and carrying torches.

Thyrsus, a kind of javelin. See Bacchus.

Tiberius, Claudius Nero, Roman emperor descended from the

Claudii. In his early days he entertained the populace with magnificent shows and gladiatorial exhibitions. Later he retired to the island of Capreae, where he indulged in vice and drunkenness. He died after a reign of twenty-two years, aged seventy-eight.

Tibullus, Aulus Albius, Roman knight famous for poetical compositions. Four books of his elegies remain.

Tides, see Naryanan.

Time (or Saturn), husband of Virtue and father of Truth.

Timoleon, famous Corinthian, son of Timodemus and Demariste. When the Syracusans, oppressed with the tyranny of Dionysius the Younger, solicited aid from the Corinthians, Timoleon sailed to Syracuse with a small fleet. His expedition was successful, and Dionysius gave himself up as prisoner.

Timon, an Athenian, called the Misanthrope from his aversion to mankind.

Timotheus, famous musician in the time of Alexander the Great.

Tiresias, famous prophet of Thebes. Juno deprived him of sight, and, in recompense, Jupiter bestowed on him the gift of prophecy.

Tisiphone, one of the Furies, daughter of Nox and Acheron.

Titanes. The Titans, name given to the gigantic sons of Coelus and Terra. The most conspicuous of them were Saturn, Hyperion, Oceanus, Iapetus, Cottus, and Briareus. They supported Titan, the elder brother of Saturn, in his war against Saturn and Jupiter.

Tithonus, husband of Aurora. At the request of his wife the gods granted him immortality, but she forgot to ask that he should be granted perpetual youth. He grew old and decrepit, while Aurora remained as fresh as the morning. The gods changed him into a grasshopper, which is supposed to moult as it grows old, and grows young again.

Titus Vespasianus, son of Vespasian and Flavia Domitilla, renowned for his valour, particularly at the siege of Jerusalem. He died A.D. 81, aged forty-one.

Tityus, son of Jupiter. A giant who was cast into the innermost hell for insulting Diana. He, like Prometheus, has a vulture constantly feeding on his ever-growing liver.

Toil, see Atlas.

Tombs, see Manes.

Tongue, see Tereus.

Tonitrualis, the Thunderer; a name of Jupiter.

Towers, see Cybele.

Tragedy, see Melpomene.

Trajanus, M. Ulpius Crinitus, Roman emperor born at Ithaca. His services to the empire brought him to the notice of the emperor Nerva, who adopted him, and invested him with the purple. The actions of Trajan were those of a benevolent prince. He died A.D. 117, aged sixty-four, his ashes being taken to Rome and deposited under a stately column which he had erected.

Trees, see Aristaeus.

Tribulation, see Echidna.

Tribuni Plebis, Roman magistrates in B.C. 261.

Triformis, see Tergemina.

Triptolemus, son of Oceanus and Terra, or according to some, Oeleus, king of Attica, and Neaera. He was cured of a serious illness in his youth by Ceres, with whom he became a great favourite. She taught him agriculture, and gave him her chariot drawn by dragons, in which he travelled over the earth, distributing corn to the inhabitants. Cicero mentions Triptolemus as the fourth judge in hell.

Triterica, Bacchanalian festivals.

Triton, sea deity, son of Neptune and Amphitrite. He was very powerful, and could calm the sea and abate storms at his pleasure.

Tritons, sons of Triton. They were trumpeters of the sea-deities, and were represented as mermen.

Triumviri, three magistrates appointed to govern the Roman state with absolute power.

Trivia, a name of Diana.

Trophonius, one of Jupiter's most famous oracles.

Troy, the classic poets say that the walls of this famous city were built by the magic sound of Apollo's lyre. See Dardanus, Helen, Hercules, Paris.

Trumpeters, see Tritons.

Truth, daughter of Time, because truth is discovered in the course of time. Democritus says that truth lies hidden at the bottom of a well.

Tullus Hostilius, succeeded Numa as king of Rome. He was of warlike disposition, and distinguished himself by his expedition against the people of Alba, whom he conquered.

Tutelina, a rural divinity, goddess of granaries.

Two faces, see Janus.

Typhoeus, or Typhon, monster with a hundred heads who made war against the gods, but was crushed by Jove's thunderbolt, and imprisoned under Mt. Etna.

Typhon, in Egyptian mythology, the god who tried to undo all the good work of Osiris.

Tyrtaeus, Greek elegiac poet born in Attica. Only a few fragments of his work remain.

U

Uller, the Scandinavian god who presided over archery and duels.

Ulysses, the famous king of Ithaca, son of Anticlea and Laertes, or, according to some, Sisyphus. His wife was Penelope, daughter of Icarius. He was so much endeared to her that he feigned madness to escape going to the Trojan war; this being discovered, however, he had to go. He was of great help to the Grecians, forcing Achilles from his retreat, and obtaining the charmed arrows of Hercules from Philoctetes, using them against the Trojans. He enabled Paris to shoot one of them at the heel of Achilles, and so kill that charmed warrior. On the conclusion of the war he embarked for Greece, but on his way was taken prisoner by the Cyclopes. He escaped after blinding Polyphemus, their chief. At Aeolia he obtained the winds of heaven and put them into a bag, but his companions, supposing it to contain treasure, cut the bag, thus letting out the winds which drove them straight back to Aeolia. Later he was thrown on an enchanted island, where he was exposed to the wiles of the enchantress Circe. She turned his companions into swine but Ulysses compelled her to restore them. Passing the islands of the Sirens he stopped the ears of his companions, and had himself bound to the mast, so that they escaped the allurements of the singers. Eventually he got to his own country, after an absence of twenty years. His wife Penelope was a model of constancy, for, though Ulysses had been reported dead, she would marry no one else. The adventures of Ulysses after his return from the Trojan war are the subject of Homer's Odyssey.

Undine, a water nymph, or sylph.

Unknown God, An, see Acts of the Apostles, Chapter 17.

Unxia, a name of Juno, relating to her protection of newly-married people.

Urania, daughter of Jupiter and Mnemosyne; the Muse who presided over astronomy.

Uranus, Greek name of Coelus; his descendants are sometimes termed Uranids.

Urgus, a name of Pluto, signifying the Impeller.

Ursa Major, see Calistro.

Ursa Minor, see Arcas.

Usurers, see Jani.

Utgord Loki, king of giants in Scandinavian mythology.

V

Valhalla, Scandinavian temple of immortality, inhabited by the souls of heroes slain in battle.

Valentinianus, the First, son of Gratian, raised to the throne for merit and valour. He gained victories over the Barbarians in Gaul and Africa, and punished the Quadi with severity. He broke a blood-vessel and died A.D. 375. After his death his son, Valentinian the Second, was proclaimed emperor. Maximus robbed him of his throne, but he regained it by the aid of Theodosius, emperor of the East. He was remarkable for benevolence and clemency. The third Valentinian was made emperor in his youth. On reaching maturer age he disgraced himself by violence and oppression. He was murdered A.D. 454.

Vali, Scandinavian god of archery.

Valleys, see Vallonia.

Varro, Latin author, famous for learning. He wrote five hundred books, all of which have been lost, with the exception of a treatise "De Re Rustica," and one other "De Lingua Latina." He died B.C. 28, aged eighty-eight.

Varuna, the Hindoo Neptune, represented as a white man riding on a sea-horse, carrying a club in one hand and a rope in the other.

Vedius, the same as Vejovis.

Vejovis, "Little Jupiter"; a name given to Jupiter when he appeared without his thunder.

Vengeance, see Nemesis.

Venus, one of the most famous deities of the ancients, was goddess of beauty, and mother of love. She sprang from the foam of the sea, and was carried to heaven, where all the gods admired her beauty. Jupiter gave her in marriage to Vulcan, but she intrigued with some of the gods, notably with Mars, their offspring being Hermione, Cupid, and Anteros. She later left Olympus and became enamoured of Adonis. Venus indirectly caused the Trojan war, for, when the goddess of discord had thrown amongst the goddesses the golden apple inscribed "To the fairest," Paris adjudged the apple to Venus, and she inspired him with love for Helen, wife of Menelaus, king of Sparta. Paris carried Helen off to Troy, and the Greeks pursued and besieged the city. (See Helen, Paris, Troy.) Venus is mentioned by the poets under the names of Aphrodite, Cypria, Urania, Astarte, Paphia, Cythera, and the laughter-loving goddess. Her favourite place of abode was Cyprus. Incense alone was usually offered on her altars, but if there was a victim it was a white goat. She was attended by Cupid and the Graces. Apelles' famous picture of her rising from the ocean is named Anadyomene.

Verticordia, Roman name of Venus, signifying the power of love to change the hard-hearted. The corresponding Greek name was Epistrophia.

Vertumnus, god of spring, or some say, of the seasons; the husband of Pomona, the goddess of orchards.

Vespasianus, Titus Flavius, Roman emperor of obscure descent. He began the siege of Jerusalem, which was continued by his son Titus. He died A.D. 79, aged seventy.

Vesta, daughter of Saturn and Cybele, was goddess of fire. She had the famous statue of Minerva under her special care. The Vestal Virgins kept a fire or lamp constantly burning before it.

Vestales, the Vestal Virgins were priestesses consecrated to the service of Vesta. They were required to be of good family, and free from blemish or deformity, and were under a solemn vow of chastity. See above.

Vialis, a name of Mercury, because he presided over the making of roads.

Victory, a goddess, daughter of Styx and Acheron, represented as flying through the air holding a wreath of laurels. See Nicephorus.

Vidor, a Scandinavian god, who could walk on water and in the air. The god of silence, corresponding with the classic Harpocrates.

Virgilius, Publius Maro, called prince of the Latin poets, was born at Andes, near Mantua, about seven years before Christ. He went to Rome, where he met Maecenas, and recommended himself to Augustus. His Bucolics were written in about three years; later he commenced the Georgics which is considered one of the most perfect of all Latin compositions. The Aeneid is supposed to have been undertaken at the request of Augustus. Virgil died, B.C. 19, aged fifty-one.

Virginia, daughter of the centurion L. Virginius. She was slain by her father to save her from the violence of the decemvir, Appius Claudius.

Virginius, valiant Roman, father of Virginia. The story of Virginius and his ill-fated daughter is the subject of the well-known tragedy of "Virginius," one of the productions of J. Sheridan Knowles.

Vulcania, Roman festivals in honour of Bacchus, at which the victims were thrown into the fire and burned to death.

Vulcanus, the god of fire, and patron of those who worked in iron. According to Homer, he was son of Jupiter and Juno, and was so deformed that at his birth his mother threw him into the sea, where he remained nine years. Other writers differ. He married Venus at the instigation of Jupiter. He is known by the name of Mulciber. The Cyclopes were his attendants, and with them he forged the thunderbolts of Jupiter.

W

War, see Bellona, Chemos, Mars.

Water, see Canopus.

Water-Nymphs, see Doris.

Wax Tablets, see Calliope.

Wealth, see Cuvera.

Weaving, see Ergatos.

Weeding, see Runcina.

Weights and Measures, see Mercury.

Well, see Truth.

West Wind, see Favonius.

Winds, see Aurora, Auster, Boreas, Zephyr.

Wine, see Bacchus, Suradevi.

Wisdom, see Pollear, Minerva.

Woden, Anglo-Saxon form of the Scandinavian god Odin; Wednesday is called after him.

Women's Safeguard, see Sospita.

Woodpecker, see Picus.

Woods, see Dryads.

World, see Chaos.

X

Xanthippe, or Xantippe, wife of Socrates, remarkable for ill-humour. She was a constant torment to her husband; on one occasion after bitterly reviling him, she emptied a vessel of dirty water over him, on which the philosopher coolly remarked, "After thunder rain generally falls."

Xanthus, name of Achilles' famous horse.

Xenocrates, an ancient philosopher born at Calcedonia, and educated in the school of Plato, whose friendship he gained. He died B.C. 314.

Xenophon, famous Athenian, son of Gryllus, was a celebrated general, philosopher, and historian. He joined Cyrus the Younger in an expedition against Artaxerxes, king of Persia, and after the decisive battle of Cunaxa, in which Cyrus was defeated and killed, the skill and bravery of Xenophon became conspicuous. He had to direct an army of ten thousand Greeks, who were now more than six hundred leagues from home, in a country surrounded by an active enemy. He surmounted all difficulties till the famous "Retreat of the Ten Thousand" was effected; the Greeks returned after a march of two hundred and fifteen days. Xenophon employed his pen in describing the expedition of Cyrus in his work, "The Anabasis." He also wrote "Cyropaedia," "Memorabilia," "Hellenica," etc. He died about B.C. 360 at Corinth, aged ninety.

Xerxes, succeeded his father Darius on the Persian throne. He entered Greece with an enormous army, which was checked at Thermopylae by the valour of three hundred Spartans under King Leonidas, who for three days successfully opposed the immense forces of Xerxes, and were at last slain. From this period the fortunes of Xerxes waned. His fleet being defeated at Salamis, and mortified by ill-success, he hastened to Persia, where he gave himself to debauchery, and was murdered about B.C. 464, aged twenty-one.

Y

Yama, the Hindoo devil, represented as a terrible green monster, with flaming eyes.

Ygdrasil, famous ash-tree of Scandinavian mythology, under which the gods held daily council.

Ymir, Scandinavian god, corresponding to Chaos of the classics.

Youth, perpetual, see Tithonus.

Z

Zama, town in Numidia, famous as the scene of the victory of Scipio over Hannibal, B.C. 202.

Zeno, famous philosopher, founder of the sect of Stoics, was born at Citium in Cyprus. He started a school in Athens, soon being noticed by the great and learned. His life was devoted to sobriety and moderation. He died, B.C. 264, aged ninety-eight.

Zeno, philosopher of Elea or Velia, in Italy. He was the disciple or, according to some, the adopted son of Parmenides. Being tortured to cause him to reveal his confederates in a plot he had engaged in, he bit off his tongue that he might not betray his friends.

Zenobia, famous princess of Palmyra, wife of Odenatus. After the death of her husband the emperor Aurelian declared war against her. She took the field with seven hundred thousand men, and although at first successful, she was eventually subdued. Aurelian treated her with great humanity. She was admired for her literary talents as well as military ability.

Zephyr, god of flowers, son of Aeolus and Aurora, the west wind. See Favonius.

Zetes, with Calais, his brother, drove the Harpies from Thrace.

Zethus, brother of Amphion. See Amphion.

Zeus, Greek name of Jupiter.

Zeuxis, famous painter, born at Heraclea. He flourished 468 B.C. He painted some grapes so naturally that the birds came to peck them on the canvas. He, himself, was disgusted with the picture, because the man depicted carrying the grapes was not natural enough to frighten the birds.

Zoilus, Sophist and grammarian of Amphipolis, B.C. 259. He became known by his severe criticisms of the works of Isocrates and Homer.

Zoroaster, king of Bactria, supposed to have lived in the time of Ninus, king of Assyria, some time before the Trojan war. He was famous for his deep researches in philosophy. He admitted no visible object of devotion save fire, which he considered the proper emblem of a Supreme Being. He was respected by his subjects and contemporaries for his abilities as a monarch, a lawgiver, and a philosopher, and, though many of his doctrines may seem puerile, he had many disciples. The religion of the Parsees was founded by Zoroaster.

Zosimus, Greek historian, living about 410 A.D. He wrote a history of some of the Roman emperors. He indulged in malevolent and vituperative attacks on the Christians in his History of Constantine.